# CINEMA DRAMA SCHEMA
## Eastern Metaphysic
## in Western Art

# *CINEMA*
# *DRAMA*
# *SCHEMA*
## *Eastern Metaphysic in Western Art*

Hector Currie

Philosophical Library
New York

**Library of Congress Cataloging In Publication Data**
Currie, Hector.
  Cinema drama schema

  Bibliography: p.
  1. Tragedy—Addresses, essays, lectures.  2. Moving-
pictures—Addresses, essays, lectures.  3. Metaphysics—
Addresses, essays, lectures.  I. Title.
PN1892.C8  1985        809.2'512        84-20771
ISBN 0-8022-2461-X

For Mother

# *Contents*

## CINEMA

## SCHEMA

...celestial mathematics
...inspired...forms...

> Joseph Campbell
> *Myths to Live By*
> (New York: Viking Press, 1972), p. 243.

...inspired mathematics [of the] emotions.

> Ezra Pound
> *The Spirit of Romance*
> (London: J. Dent, 1910; Norfolk, Va.:
> J. Laughlin, 1952), p. 14.

# *Acknowledgments*

"The Energies of Tragedy" appeared in Michigan State University's *Centennial Review*; "The Strange Pedantry of William Rowley in *The Changeling*" in *Revue d'Histoire du Theatre* (Paris); "*Riders to the Sea* Reappraised" in the University of Texas *Texas Quarterly*; "The Surprising Unconscious of Edward Albee" in the University of Minnesota's *Drama Survey*; and "The Schematized Vision of Josef von Sternberg in *Blonde Venus* was broadcast on the Voice of America's Film Forum series. The article on Jean-Luc Godard is a revision of one that appeared in the *Journal of Modern Literature*. "Encounter with Essence: The Schematic Image" appeared in the *Journal of the University Film Association*.

*SCHEMA*

# Introduction

The schematism by which [we understand] the
world is deeply hidden.[1]
Immanuel Kant

Our lives are ragged. We long for order. Man's long history of
art, and science, is a record of his search for order in the
seeming chaos that is life.

Structure is the objective of our studies of the art image and
of natural phenomena. Modern man has discovered an order
to the cosmos and the atom. Nature has achieved a structure in
the mind of man. Yet there remains, in the unbridled psyche,
the threat of annihilation to all we have achieved.

This work is offered as a testament to man's genius for order,
in the hope that its discoveries of the order structuring works of

---

[1] Immanuel Kant, *Kritik der reinen Vernunft*, in E.H. Gombrich, *Art and
Illusion*, (Princeton, N.J.: Princeton University Press, 1960), p. 63.

3

art may give solace to the troubled spirit as, to borrow from Matthew Arnold's dark vision, "ignorant armies clash by night."[2]

Arnold—his work bears on this present endeavor: he believed that art, literature, could elevate the spirit and deliver it from the heavy press of materialism which burdened his age of the machine as it now burdens our age of electronic information. And, in his studies, Arnold looked to the inceptive center of Western culture for guidance to free us of the sea of despond, looked to the creator of the epic, to Homer.

To Homer—the Ionian.

Ionia—bridge between Classical Greece and the East; home of the great natural philosopher, Anaximander (c. 610-545 BC).

Anaximander—it is the thesis of this study that Anaximander, with Pythagoras of Samos (c. 560-c. 480 BC), was the inspirator of the Greek concept of cosmic order that gave order to tragic form.

The connection may strike the reader as an eccentric quirk; the study of Greek tragedy has, in the past, compartmentalized art and science, and, it is my contention, has failed to discern the amazing concordance that exists between Anaximander's concept of being and the realization of the cosmic schema structuring all that exists—and the Greek theater.

In his study of Anaximander's cosmology, Charles S. Kahn notes that Anaximander "was the first to depict...Delphi,...the navel of earth,...at the center."[3] This deserves heavy emphasis in a study of the origins of Greek theater, for Delphi, not Athens, was the center of Greek religion, and tragedy was a religious ritual.

---

[2] Matthew Arnold, "Dover Beach."

[3] Charles S. Kahn, *The Encyclopedia of Philosophy*, (New York: Macmillan, 1967), p. 117.

Thus, in seeking for evidence of a structural order in the Greek mind, where better to look than the cosmic center, Delphi?

Here, at Delphi, at the center, we have the fusion of Apolline and Dionysiac ritual that joins West and East.

Here at Delphi we have the geometrizing of time and space that is the mark of structural analysis and synthesis. At Delphi we shall find the order of the templum and theater complex to be based on the power of number, the power of the numbers three and four which, added, as numerology dictates, equal the number sacred to Apollo, "Captain of Sevens." It shall be the burden of the exposition of this schema which is to follow to suggest that the Greek philosopher Anaximander conceived of this combination of numbers—their factored powers, three to the fourth power—as the key to his cosmic scheme, and, further, that Pythagoras applied this uniting of the powers of space and time to his design for the Delphic seat.

In brief, it is here proposed that Delphi is not the jumble of buildings that it has been deemed by archeologists. Rather, it is a launching pad for the spirit; an intricately devised spatial ordering of temple and theater that projects Apollo's arrow from the cosmic center into infinity.

Again, the reader may feel that this violates the Apolline principle of limit: "Know the mean—the limit." But, it might be asked, does such a narrow view of the Greek spirit take into account the Eastern metaphysic of Dionysus? And, it must be constantly kept in mind, Dionysus shared the Delphic center with Apollo for one quarter of the year.

Anaximander's concept of the Boundless—this, it is here maintained, is the counterpoise to the Delphic limit.

Greek tragedy did not celebrate death, but transcendence, transcendence through form.

And the theater and temple at Delphi demonstrate topographically this divine order of limit-and-release.

Consult the diagram in Chapter 1 (Figure 1, p. 10).

Note the two tripods which relate centers and thresholds, permanence and change, stasis and dynamis.

Note how man, in approaching the sacred shrine, standing on the Great Path before the temple, is at one extremity of the tripod centering in the temple's *omphalos*, with its other termini at the center of the theater and in the Temple of the Athenians (consecrated to Athena).

Note, further, approaching to the base of the ramp fronting the temple, that this threshold centering at the entrance to the adyton, the inner sanctum, finds, in this tripod of thresholds, termini at the central door of the theater's stage house, and at the threshold of the mound of Earth (she, the first "god"—goddess—at the Delphic seat).

Further, observe that the orientation of the temple is along the East-West axis, if the orientation of the temple be considered in the form of a seven-pointed star (of six points and a seventh in the center).

The original motive that led to the investigation of the topological order at Delphi was that, at the temple's center, a tripod was (or so tradition deemed it) poised over a cleft in the earth. Seated on this tripod was the priestess as she received inspiration for utterances that were transcribed in hexameter.

Then, once the spatial order had been discerned, attention was given the temporal aspect; and as noted, $3^4$—the third raised to the fourth power/dimension—led to the association of Anaximander's cosmic scheme. For Anaximander, who, as noted, placed his cosmic center at Delphi, sought, in his cosmology (according to Furley and Allen[4]), "a sense of aesthetic symmetry.... The intervals between each of the infinite worlds are equal.... Earth and sun are equal.... Asia and Europe are equal." And the divine number was $3^4=81$: the ratio of the earth's depth to the circle of the sun.

---

[4] David J. Furley and R.E. Allen, *Studies in Presocratic Philosophy*, I (London: Routledge and Kegan Paul, 1970), p. 75.

Pythagoras, an initiate of the Delphic shrine, was to realize this divine number in his sacred *tetractys*. In it are to be found eighty-one geometric figures, triangles, diamonds, and a hexagon.

The fourth dimension is the key to Delphi ($3^4=81$), for it was the seat of prophecy.

And that brings us to what, I feel, is the most staggering discovery at the center; the theater and temple are related by the astral wheel of the zodiac! The stars wheel above Dionysus in perfect order, with one twelfth of the circle of the year moving into the house of Apollo, bringing the powers of the signs to bear on the center of Greek worship. Such an Eastern infusion—is it to be credited? It most assuredly is; Anaximander was from the meeting place of East and West, and it was he who brought the Zodiac and the *gnomon* (the sundial) to Greece.

Would it strain credibility too far to suggest that the theater of Dionysus, just as it was the center of the night skies, was also a center of the solar whirl? For the two *periaktoi*, three-sided scenic devices that flanked the stage, may be seen to cast shadows toward the theater's center in a quartile division of the sun's course reaching its zenith at noon along the *periaktoi*-sundial's southern axis. The passage of time, this marked the inexorable movement of the tragic hero toward his fate. Dionysus, it bears stressing, is time, moving, as Apollo is space, spatial order, *and* the transcendence of space/time.

Should any doubt the order of the diagram, it might be noted that the coincidence of the southeast axis of the zodiac at precisely the termini of the tripod legs at the threshold of Earth and at the Temple of the Athenians—which also is the point of intersection with the path of the great circle tracing the Great Path of approach to the shrine—would appear to erase any such doubts. This achievement of topographic survey, on the irregularly sloping ground of the templum, suggests only one possible architect—Pythagoras.

And, in these termini, in shrines to Earth and Athena we have realized an historic conspectus: the movement from worship of earth's powers to those of the world. Such can only be considered a descent in motive. It would seem that the architect conceived of the temporality of his creation. It survived a millennium, but, with the defeat of the vision of Julian ("the Apostate"), the fire at the altar of Greek culture went out.

It is the hope of this study that its fire might once again inspire man to see beyond the limit of death to the transcendent Boundless of Anaximander.

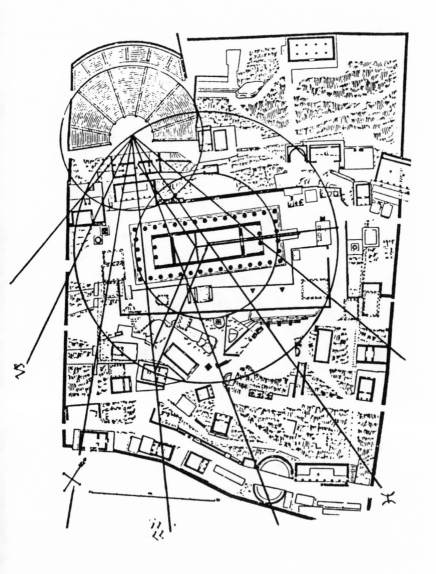

*Figure 1.* Delphi. (Source: see ref. 5.)

# Inceptive Schema:
## Delphi and Philadelphia
### (with Michael Porte)

As Noam Chomsky has observed: "an innate schematism"[1]
structures experience, providing the equipoise between the
opposing factors of change and permanence that so intrigued
the first Western philosophers, the pre-Socratics.

To Heraclitus, herald of change, becoming was the cardinal
principle of existence: "All is flux."

To Parmenides, the center of being was to be found in an
unchanging unity of existence.

In this regard, within the temple of Apollo at Delphi, at the
center of the Greek world, lay an object, the navel stone
(*omphalos*), possessing a deep and dual meaning which
encompassed both the oneness of the source and the duality of
the shared home of the two gods of the Greek pantheon
embodying the opposed forces of mind and nature: Apollo,

---

[1] Ben Rothblatt, ed., *Changing Perspectives on Man* (Chicago; University
of Chicago Press, 1968), pp. 7-8.

11

god of idea and austere Parmenidean form, and Dionysus, god of nature in all its fecund Heraclitian change.

The temple of Apollo—and of Dionysus, for one quarter of the year, the winter months—was a seat of prophecy, it being both the pivotal point of the Greek cosmos and, as well, a temporal vantage point for projective vision into the future.

And that inspired vision from the mantic seat set forth a dynamic order that symbolizes the equipoise of Dionysiac impulse and Apollonian concept, emotion and logic, inspiration and judgment.

Here, at Delphi, we find permanence and change, Apollo and Dionysus, in harmonious concord. The ordering of energies evident in the plan of the temple could stand as a dynamic diagram of man's spiritual quest for order, and for release from spatial and temporal constraints into a transcendence of material limit; this, paradoxically, at the sacred seat bearing above the temple's portal Apollo's motto: "Know the limit."

Consulting the templum plan (Figure 1), an intricate spatial pattern emerges.

At the center of the Greek cosmos the navel stone of earth is situated. About it, the circle encompassing Apollo's temple is matched, in a perfect symmetry, by the circle encompassing the theater of Dionysus.

Also, symbolic symmetry is present in the seven quadrantal lines radiating from the center of the theater, seven being the number sacred to Apollo, he "the Captain of Sevens," master of the harmony of the spheres on his seven-stringed lyre as, upon it, he sounded the triadic chord. The seven radiant lines will be seen to structure three zodiacal signs—Capricorn, Aquarius, and Pisces—which were, such is the exactitude with which the temple contains precisely one zodiacal house, resident in the temple while Dionysus resided within the navel stone during Apollo's three-month wintry absence.

The symbolic significance of the zodiacal wheeling of the firmament radiating from Dionysus' theater and penetrating Apollo's seat of order is the theme of change within permanence.

As noted, the quadrant radiating from the center of the theater of Dionysus constitutes a quarter of the annual turning of the zodiac in the night skies. According to T.B.L. Webster,[2] Anaximander has been credited with introducing the zodiac to Greece. We shall have more to say about Anaximander's intimate connection to the mysteries of Delphi shortly.

Plato, in the *Timaios*, hinted at this aspect of the dynamic celestial order centering in the orchestra of Dionysus' theater:

> The choric dance of stars...send upon
> men...things which will come to pass.[3]

Such an astral imperative, present in the triadic division of the winter quarter of Dionysus' residence at Delphi, is also borne out by the trieteric rite celebrated at Delphi wherein the sacrificial god of tragedy, Dionysus, suffered division into three parts.[4]

Such is the temporal order imposed by the zodiac on Apollo's templum.[5]

Beyond the limits of time, there is a relative dimensionality at Delphi which bears out the first extant ordering of the cosmos, the cosmic scheme of Anaximander, it having fixed the ratio of the depth of earth to the distant sun as one to eighty-one.

Apollo's sacred number is seven.

Three to the fourth power (the third, carried to the fourth dimension) is eighty-one.

And Pythagoras, an initiate of the Delphic mysteries, he

---

[2] T.B.L. Webster, *Athenian Culture and Society* (Berkeley; University of California Press, 1973), p. 243.

[3] Jack Lindsay, *Origins of Astrology* (New York; Barnes & Noble, 1971), p. 91.

[4] Lewis Richard Farnell, *The Cults of the Greek States* (Oxford; Clarendon Press, 1909), p. 177.

[5] Spyros Meletzis and Helen Papadakis, *Delphi* (Munich; Schnell and Steiner, 1968), p. vii.

having sojourned one year at Apollo's sacred seat, and while there having "revolutionized the art of prophecy;"[6] whose followers put number against Anaximander's concept of "the boundless" and called "...the combination of the two...harmony," he, Pythagoras, also made eighty-one his, inasmuch as there are geometric figures (triangles, diamonds, and a hexagon) numerologically totaling 81 contained within the figure sacred to the Pythagorean brotherhood.

13  triangles   x 3 = 39
 9  diamonds    x 4 = 36
 1  hexagon     x 6 =  6

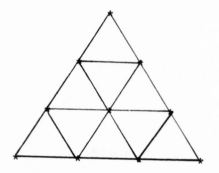

Again, an Anaximandrian spatial ordination is to be found at Delphi: consider the comparative distances between temple and theater, threshold of temple to its center, and threshold of stagehouse central door to the reach of Dionysus' thespian realm; they will be found to bear a relationship of precisely three to one, the relationship Anaximander set as the ratio of earth to underworld. The concordance is striking, for it suggests the action of the tragic trilogy and satyr play, a journey of descent and ascent for Orphic Dionysus, nature god of sacrifice and vernal rebirth.

Rebirth; we are, with this concept, still within the confines of time.

  [6] C.J. Vogel, *Pythagoras and Early Pythagoreanism* (Assen; Van Gorcum, 1966), p. 242.

Where, then, is to be found the element of "transcendence" at Delphi?

Recalling the advice of Heraclitus—Apollo, "the Slantwise Interpreter, neither speaks nor conceals but gives signs" (fr. 18)—we might consider the "signs" by which Apollo speaks and find in Apollo's tripod and arrow, he "the Far-Darter," the key to Delphi's transcendent dimension.

At the cosmic center, a tripod stood above the cleft of earth, or so legend has it. Schematically, it might be viewed as a triform arrow, with a fourth point at its tensional center. Thus visualized, the tripod may be conceived as having a projectile function. A three-dimensional object in space, possessing a projective thrust, it might thus be viewed as a schema of the fourth dimension (three to the fourth power). To resort to contemporary terminology, the temple was a "launching pad" and the tripod an Apollo spacecraft, vaulting into space, and, as Pioneer 10 has demonstrated, breaking free into the vast intergalactic void. Anaximander would have appreciated this achievement of NASA, for he, in a most un-Greek extravagance, conceived of the primal root of all to be "the boundless."

Are we to imagine he conceived of this extension with no thought of the "bound" nature of the Greek mind, as realized in myth and actuality—in the temple complex at Delphi? Did he not place the center of his symmetric world—Europe and Asia in perfect equipoise—at Delphi? Upon this center of limit he imposed the infinite reach of his mind—a reach that sought to extend beyond the tragic press of existence he felt all too well, as one may glean from his profound framing of the tragic equation:

> All things arise out of the boundless
> and make reparation to one another
> for the injustices they commit—
> according to time.

Anaximander was from Miletus, from Asia Minor. His thinking, and sensing, had an Asian cast.

What all this comes down to is simply this: will the Western mind once again open to the East?

Is it ready once again to consider the center, deeply, finding within, at the central point, no final point?

Delphi is now a quiet ruin, its dust stirred only by the idle feet of "packaged-tour" vacationists and their unenlightened tour guides. It stands as silent testimony to the veracity of Anaximander's tragic vision, as framed by Werner Jaeger:

> ...coming to be and passing away...
> Anaximander's eternal scheme...[7]

The flame is out.

Is it possible to rekindle the spark?

Some few years ago, in the middle of the dispirited seventies, our nation celebrated its Bicentennial. The flame of freedom did not then catch fire. But, marking the occasion, a most remarkable book was issued by the Department of State, *The Great Seal of the United States*.[8]

Here we had at hand an explication of the historic development of a vital symbol, the "dynamic...symbol" Peter Drucker termed essential for the rallying of great enterprise.[9]

And the symbol was born in Philadelphia:

Phila-delphi-a

This is, quite literally, love of brothers ("The City of Brotherly

---

[7] Werner Jaeger, *Paideia*, tr. Gilbert Highet (New York; Oxford University Press, 1945), pp. 160-61.

[8] Department of State, *The Great Seal of the United States* (Washington; U.S. Government Printing Office, 1976).

[9] Peter F. Drucker, *Concept of the Corporation* (New York; John Day and Company, 1946 & 1972), p. 7.

Love")—from the same womb, *"delphi,"* the dolphin being a womb symbol.

Apollo and Dionysus, sharing Semele's womb at Delphi? The framers of our Constitution, might they not have sensed that they were joining the opposed forces of the dolphin when they wrought this hallowed document? The dolphin, an arc of light in the sun, bearing Dionysus to safety on its back, aspirant, rising as the two eagles which met at the zenith over Delphi, and falling back into the waters; is this not a symbol of all high enterprise—for the process is repeated—the dolphin makes yet another arc, ever seeking to attain the sun. "The eternal scheme" (Jaeger) of aspiration, of hope in the future, in a future of freedom; might these concepts not have been in the minds of our forefathers in Philadelphia in the spring of '76? The story of the Great Seal suggests that, indeed, such was the case.

For, throughout the account of the birth of the American republic, one concept comes to the fore—the concept of leadership. And, more remarkable still, a sub-theme of mystery.

First, as to the theme of leadership: many ideas were proposed for the face of the Seal. Franklin proposed Moses, a leader of his people; Adams, Hercules, valiant hero and leader; Jefferson, a cloud by day and pillar of fire by night, leading the children of Israel in the wilderness.

Finally, in 1782, the committee settled on a symbol of independence, initiative, the American bald eagle, rising, astride a crest, and bearing an olive branch in its right talon and a bundle of arrows in its left.

The history of the reverse of the Seal is bathed in deep mystery, it being a fourscore accretion (1776-1856) of mystic symbolism.

In 1776 at the behest of the triumviral committee of Franklin, Adams and Jefferson, Du Simitière sketched the radiant triangle which, in 1856, was to enclose the Eye (in a July *Harper's Magazine* article-and-sketch by Benson J. Lossing.

*Figure 2.*    Benson J. Lossing design for the reverse of The Great
Seal, in *Harper's Magazine,* July, 1856.

See Figure 2). The thirteen-step unfinished pyramid, above
which the mystic Eye gleams, came from Francis Hopkinson's
design of 1778 for the Continental Congress's fifty-dollar bill.

The thirteen-tiered unfinished pyramid, representing the
original thirteen states and their status of incompletion until
the framing of the unitive Constitution, may be seen as akin to
the unanswered Riddle of the Sphinx, addressed to Oepidus in
his search for identity: "What walks on four feet in the morning, two at noon, and three at night?"

The series 4, 2, 3, cries for completion in the integer 1, i.e.,
man; just as the pyramid of states cried for the unity of the
federal constitution. This symbolic form may be seen as
schematically equivalent to the Pythagorean *tetractys*, a
pyramid/triangle with 4, 3, 2, 1, as its rising order. The "one" at
the apex of this holiest schema, might it not be the all-seeing
eye within the radiant triangle that caps the unfinished

pyramid on The Great Seal of the United States? It is the eye of man, of the free man gifted with vision of his, and his nation's, destiny.

Further, beyond this Oedipal deep in the emblem of the Great Seal, there is deep mystery to its motto. Selected by Secretary of the Continental Congress Charles Thomson in 1782, it is from a "pagan" poet, from Virgil:

> *Novus ordo seclorum*
> "A new secular order"
> *Eclogue*, IV

This is the base inscription.

And, inscribed above the radiant eye within the triangle, yet another Virgilian motto:

> *Annuit coeptis*
> "Favor daring undertakings."

This is a prayer. To a Roman god, to Jupiter? But, and this bears great emphasis, *without* a subject, with the god left out, so that the power is to be inferred.

The pyramid, the radiant triangle bearing the Eye (of Horus?)—all suggest solar rituals of ancient Egypt. The radiant Eye, rising, is a call for visionary leadership, for initiatives that serve a high purpose.

And, the mystery deepening, the Eye became, with Benson Lossing's vivid design of 1856 (see Figure 2), the *left* eye, which, in heraldic terms, is the eye sinister of Venus, or Satan. Lest this be taken as a glancing argument for an insidious demonic plot at the root of our most hallowed Seal of State, close study of the design will reveal a formal cause for the shift from dexter to sinister in the Eye: Lossing gave the pyramid a three-dimensional form, and oriented it toward the right; the left eye, then, looks left across a right-facing pyramid. In effect, the thrusts of pyramid and Eye intersect, creating a poised tension in the design.

Result—figuratively, the mysterious energies of Eye and pyramid drive the engine of State, fueling its "daring undertakings."

Closer to our (prosaic) day, Vice-President Henry Agar Wallace proposed to FDR in the Thirties that the Seal be put on the reverse of $1 bill, and President Roosevelt insisted that the pyramid-Eye be moved to the left side, under the legend, "The Great Seal..."

Thus, at the base of its currency system our nation proclaims the entrepreneurial principle:

> ...daring undertakings

The concept is epic in scope. It brings to mind the greatest epic spirit, Homer:

> And what he greatly thought, he nobly dared.
> *Odyssey*, II, tr. Alexander Pope

Stand beside the Liberty Bell. Look far to your right. Rising in the distance—can you make it out? That impressive structure? There, on Independence Mall, we have the United States Mint.

Consult Figure 3, Philadelphia. Note that you are situated at the energic center of the thrust from the Judicial branch (the Federal Courthouse) and the Executive (Washington Square), through the crucial agency of the Legislative (Independence Hall), that points toward Trade (the Custom House).

The U.S. Mint, as at Delphi, forms the fulcrum to yet a second home of "the twins" within the *omphalos*. It has the triadic shaping of symbolic forces, joining the thrusts of industry (Franklin Square) and government (Independence Hall), through the agency of our free-enterprise system (the U.S.

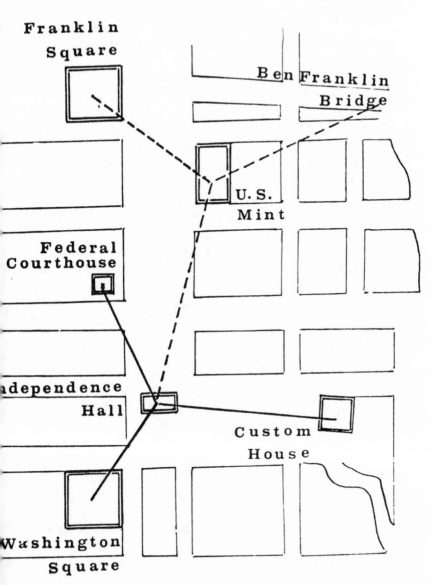

*Figure 3.*   Philadelphia.

Mint), in a projective thrust toward a joint meeting of minds (and fortunes) in the symbol of unitive purpose, a bridge (the Ben Franklin).

Admittedly, the triadic schema may be seen to have undergone a sea change in the New World. To the Greek world at Delphi, at its cosmic center, the fixity of Apollonian principle and the flux of Dionysiac impulse found realization in a tripod/arrow and, above them, in the wheel of the stars/zodiac. It was a schema of transcendence, of the Anaximandrian "boundless." Whereas, at Philadelphia, at the seat of government, the ordering of the triune forces of the Republic—executive, legislative, and judicial—and of Commerce—technological, financial, and governmental—was of a worldly cast.

To those attuned to spiritual vibrations, these schemata—one, transcendently Idealistic; the other, commercially interactive—are paradigms of civilization's long descent from Olympian *arêté* (excellence) to worldly enterprise.

Yet, however great the descent, how much greater has been our further descent from these visions of destiny to our present obeisance to the binary logic of the computer.

In this "age of information," have we lost, quite, the metaphysical urge?

Can modern man rediscover the springing thrust of number which animated the Pythagorean school? Can we sense the flux of Heraclitus in the seeming stasis of Parmenides, the movement of change in the seeming stillness of order? Can we find again the sacral dynamic of Delphi—Dionysus and Apollo, the warring aspects of the psyche, transcendent in the Anaximandrian *apeiron*?

Can man regain the vision that breaks the bond of limit, of number, and find release in the all-cancelling, limitless reaches of the mind?

This is the lesson to be learned from the transcendent schemata at the source, the inceptive schemata shaped in the stones of Delphi.

And at Philadelphia, at freedom's fount, another lesson to be learned from the mystic schema we carry about with us and pass from hand to hand. Etched in green we see rising the proud eagle, and, rising in light, the Eye, the Eye of Great Daring.

*DRAMA*

# The Energies of Tragedy

Energy is eternal delight.
William Blake

## I.

The rushlight of tragic theory, the flame of tragedy—both dead. Or so the existential consensus would have us believe. From such vantage points giving on "the human condition" as ashcans, earth-mounds, and sandboxes (we here except Eliot's ant-hill), one might glean that, indeed, the fire within is out, if there ever had been such a fire. Viewed from the mundane perspective of today's dominant genre of tragifarce, the tragic impulse appears to be nothing more than a ludicrous delusion.

Yet acquiescence in the prevailing malaise of this purported age of alienation and disbelief has not been complete. Hard though it be to credit their presence in a world of social uplift and private collapse, isolated dissents against the fashionable

27

philosophies of despair and decay have been registered. In the works of Nietzsche, Strindberg, and Jung, we find undecayed, charged particles of human and suprahuman force, particles which meet in an archetypal opposition, from whence issues the parapsychic isotope of the energic process of drama on the ultimate plane—the dazzling dark of cosmic tragedy.

Deriving from Vedic philosophy and Jungian mythic study, the cosmic transcendence theory of tragedy which is here advanced strives to integrate such evidences of tragic affirmation as are discoverable in the works of Goethe, Nietzsche, Strindberg, and Artaud in a pan-cultural and transcendent matrix for cosmic tragedy. It identifies tragedy's ultimate action as an integration of the psyche of the hero in the cosmic energy of original chaos. Conceiving an integrative action to be the consummation of the tragic hero's passion, it extends the bounds of tragic action beyond the conventional act of psychic (and physical) separation to include the act of cosmic transcendence. This conception of tragedy as an ultimately integrative action on a cosmic plane is conducive to the effect of Longinian sublimity induced by transcendent action.

In defense of this inclusion of action of cosmic transcendence in the tragic canon, it is here maintained that tragedy, the highest form of dramatic expression, cannot be limited to an emotionally purgative psychic tragedy of stress but must encompass the furthest reaches of experience—the sublime, the ultimate, the transcendent. Furthermore, inasmuch as all these metaphysical qualities exceed human powers of rational comprehension, tragedy, it follows, must be accepted as irrational (at least to Western consciousness), as having a mystic dimensionality which projects beyond the bounds of ordering reason. Confronted by *Oedipus at Colonus* and *The Dream Play*, we are driven to admit their cosmic extension; surely reason, with its linear phasing of action into a time sequence terminating in a catastrophe and its two-dimensional weighing of situations and characters on the subjective scales of "good" and "evil," cannot cope with their mysteries. Nor is an intellectually arrived at cathexis in an equilibrant purging of the emotions—Aristotle's concept of catharsis—able to penetrate the veils obscuring their tragic essence. Indeed, Aristotle, in his discussion of "The Supernatural," interdicts the cosmic level in tragedy: "In the incidents there should be nothing inexplicable." However, in discussing "The Epic: The Marvelous and Inexplicable," this interdiction is seemingly lifted: "Tragedy should make men marvel, but the epic...has greater scope for the inexplicable." Nietzsche, in his high Romantic efflorescences, in *The Birth of Tragedy*, was not one to scant the cosmic level: "In *Oedipus at Colonus*...we have here a transcendent serenity...hinting that by his passive endurance the hero may yet gain a consummate energy of action." And this is based on Nietzsche's mystic philosophy of tragedy at the cosmic level, whereat "the spell of individuation," "the root of all evil," "...may yet be broken, as an augury of eventual integration."

Nietzsche was not alone in his faith in the transcendent nature of tragedy: Goethe, Strindberg, Jung, and Artaud also had faith, variously framed but essentially one in affirmative tone, in modern man's capacity to attain supranatural heights and depths. The cosmic transcendence (integration with original chaos) theory of tragedy has drawn heavily upon their insights, and is sustained by their faith.


## II. The Search for the Source

The great merit of the romantic attitude in poetry, and of the transcendental method in philosophy is that they put us back at the beginning of our experience. They disintegrate convention, which is often cumbrous and confused, and restore us to ourselves, to immediate perception and primordial will. That, as it would seem, is the true and inevitable starting point.

"The inevitable starting point." Santayana's statement, in *Three Philosphical Poets*, made with reference to the inspirational source of the creative process, by extension, could, in the context of tragedy, apply as well to the creative outcome, the tragic action: the creative artist, the tragic hero, both seek the source. And, granting the poet's (hero's) return to the source as the purpose informing the action, and the end toward which he strives, what, then, might be implied by Santayana's "beginning of our experience...[which restores us to] primordial will," *the* source, and objective, of the creative-tragic impulse? The defining of "beginning" will reveal the nature of the root source of the cosmic transcendence theory of tragedy.

Were the theory founded on a nontranscendent ground, the beginning could find its source in human experience: personal emergence from the womb, the Freudian inceptive point; racial emergence from the primeval darkness of the subconscious, the Jungian source of sentience. Perceptive though both concepts are, and relevant though they may be to phases of the tragic action, they are not adequate to reach the ultimate source, the generative impulse impelling transcendent tragedy. Tragedy, conceived as transcendent, subsumes more than mere human existence; it concerns more than man, encompasses all being, and nonbeing. True, man is at the center— "Man has felt," as Eliade has said in *The Sacred and the Profane*, "the need to live at the Centre always." But what is the nature of the cosmic field in which man, supremely egoistic, establishes his focal position? What is the ground of which the figure of man is but a part, and, paradoxically, the whole? The answer must necessarily be speculative. All we can do is venture possible solutions on the basis of intuition and scientifically based speculation.

Modern physics reveals that all matter originated in, and eventually will return to, energy. "Energy fields are the soul of matter," Oliver Reiser writes in *Man's New Image of Man*. Thus, in searching for the source of the tragic impulse, energy would appear to be a likely unitive source. But the term "energy," to serve in the energic field theory of tragedy, needs further refinement, for energy has many forms, not all of which are relevant in the tragic context. All energy of which we are aware is structurally ordered: atomic theories hypothesize that the constituents of energic action are charged particles whose motion is conventionally schematized in a waveform pattern. Again, with reference to the transcendent nature of tragedy, we find this concept insufficient: inherent in wave-form structure is a dualism. We must go further yet in our search for the source of the tragic-cosmic impulse. Just as we have passed beyond man, and beyond race, we must probe for an energic field beyond the configurations of subatomic waveform theory.

An energic field which is as yet invisible to scientific observation is the field of psychic energy. Unseen, yet ever present in our subconscious, the powers of the psyche are the subject of increasing psychological interest, an interest which has a long history. Greek philosophers recognized that psychic ecstasy was essential in the creative process. During the Middle Ages, studies into the dark recesses of necromancy and alchemy continued the respect for the powers of the occult evidenced by the orphic cults and other cabalistic orders in ancient Greece. The advent of Enlightenment subscription to scientific experimental method did not deter belief, among artists, in suprarational forces. Shakespeare and Webster employed psychic phenomena in their works for more than superficial theatrical effect. The Romantic movement again gave full recognition to psychic experience. Goethe wrote is his *Autobiography* with regard to his concept of daemonic powers:

> A tremendous power issues from them, and they exercise an incredible dominion over all creatures, indeed, even over the elements, and who can say how far such influence will extend. All united moral powers are of no avail against it.

"...and who can say how far such influence will extend?" The influence remarked upon by Goethe partially implies an answer. "Influence" suggests the presence of will in the psychic (daemonic) force, will: order. Thus there is inherent in psychic energy a structuring in dualistic wave-form order. Transcendent tragedy cannot have as its source ordered, dualistic phenomena, inasmuch as "order" implies an added duality: ordering agent and ordered energic outcome or cause and effect. This Goethe saw intuitively for, in his *Satyros*, he described "in untranslatable language how the first signs of order came into chaos." Here we have an answer to the question of "the beginning of our experience [which restores us to] primordial will." Here, in chaos, is the origin. In the undifferentiated flux of chaos, beyond time and existence, in the transcendence of the state of becoming which Heraclitus envisaged in his image of the all-consuming, all-creating fire; here, in transcendent chaos—"the preformal modality of cosmic matter [energy, as in the Babylonian seminal substance, *apsū*, the formless chaos before creation]...that precedes and follows life," as Eliade puts it—in this original chaos the tragic hero finds the source to which he subconsciously yearns to return, the source wherein is resolved all the tensional dichotomies and antinomies of existence.

In brief, cosmic tragedy, celebrating the transcendence of existence by the hero, returns him, through the process of self-sacrificial destruction of selfhood, to the source, eternal—original and ever-present—chaos. The tragic hero, in a transpsychic metamorphosis reintegrates his psyche with that of the cosmos, losing self and finding total identity. The timed cyclic rhythm of life, energy-matter, is transcended by the hero in a cosmic synapse. Escaping from the confines of material existence the hero attains a state of nonbeing-being, the field of cosmic energy, the whole which was violated when energy and matter separated from primal chaos, when being was cleaved from the state beyond being.

### III. The Process: Transcendent Fusion

In effect, the hero (*atman*, self) becomes "god" (*brahman*, all). As stated by Antonin Artaud:

> Transported outside and beyond himself (or what he believes to be himself, but is only an apparent and superficial aspect of his being), he is reintegrated into the universal, into what is sensible beyond the senses.
> [The transport is effected through] the burning and decisive tranfusion of matter by spirit.

What Artaud sensed at the base of tragic experience was the consuming and purifying fire, the flame at the heart of myth, source of the "blazing visions" traced in Joseph Campbell's *The Hero with a Thousand Faces*, visions of "...the radiance of a divine power which, though transcendent, is yet immanent in all things."

However, fire, light, is but half of the cosmic whole at the heart of myth; there is a correlate darkness which Western religions have repudiated as immoral. In the Western world there has been a radical separation of light and darkness, in contrast to the Eastern fusing and transcending of antagonistic forces. The fusing of oppositional creative and destructive forces in the dance of the androgynous Hindu god, Shiva (incorporating a fused dualism, as well, in one form of his female power—*shakti*—the dark goddess, the black mother, Kali, preserver-and-destroyer), wherein "...light and darkness [dance] together in a world creating [and destroying] cosmic shadow play" strikingly symbolizes the wholeness of the Eastern philosophy in contrast to the Western world's struggle to the finish between the contesting cosmic powers, with light triumphant, darkness vanquished and banished, and moral "perfection" the outcome. (It might be asked: how can there be metaphysical perfection of a part?) The compromising of opposites, an Eastern principle (the fusing of Yin and Yang in Taoism; Shiva and Shakti in Hinduism), as set forth by the pre-Socratic Greek philosopher, Heraclitus: "The unlike are joined together, and from differences result the most beautiful harmony, and all things take place by strife," has but rarely entered Western consciousness. Yet this fusing of opposites is the secret of the strange harmony proceeding from discordant energies which art of complexity and substance effects. The Western critical aesthetic, heavily freighted with rational-logical and moral impedimenta, has in the main been insensitive, if not hostile, to the resolving energies of art, to the sublimity of Heraclitus. The full dawn of psychic-aesthetic awareness in the West awaited Nietzsche's rebellion against the oppressive tradition in his celebration of the Dionysiac ecstacy in creation-destruction. R.P. Blackmur has given evidence of the penetration of Nietzsche's beam into critical consciousness. Referring to the psychic effect of "enantiodromia" produced by Yeats' "Crazy Jane Talks to the Bishop," Blackmur cites the passage:

> ...love has pitched his mansion in
> The place of excrement;
> For nothing can be sole or whole
> That has not been rent.

and remarks upon its psychic effect:

> It is an enantiodromia, the shocked condition, the turning point, where a thing *becomes* its own opposite, than which there is no place at once more terrifying and more fortifying to find oneself in.

Despite the traumatic effect of this plunge into dark nature, enantiodromia can reach only the psychic depths of tragedy; the cosmos is not to be transcended through shock: the psychic charge driving to the center, into the finitude of the self, whereas with transcendent experience the self disappears and all interfuses with a mystic gesture that is beyond the continuum of space and time. At this passage from Yeats our shudder is seated in our senses and intellects, the harmony of opposites is at the psychic level. As an instance of a harmony at the cosmic level, the messenger's speech in *Oedipus at Colonus* might be exampled:

> ...there came a silence. Then
> A voice from some one cried aloud to him,
> And filled them all with fear, that made each hair
> To stand on end. For, many a time, the God
> From many a quarter calls to him. 'Ho there.
> Come, come, thou Oedipus, why stay we yet?
> Long time thy footsteps linger on the way.'
> ...then straightaway Oedipus
> Clasping his children with his sightless hands,
> Spake thus: 'My children! Now ye need to show
> Your tempers true and noble, and withdraw
> From where ye stand, nor think it right to look
> On things that best are hidden, nor to list
> To those that speak; but yet, with utmost speed
> Go forth. But Theseus, who may claim the right,
> Let him remain, to learn the things that come.'
> So much we all together heard him speak,
> And then, with tears fast flowing, groaning still
> We followed with the maidens. Going on
> A little space we turned. And lo! we saw
> The man was no more; but he, the king was there,
> Holding his hand to shade his eyes, as one
> To whom there comes a vision drear and dread
> He may not bear to look on. Yet awhile,
> But little, and we see him bowed to earth,
> Adoring it, and in that self-same prayer
> Olympus, home of Gods. What form of death
> He died, knows no man, but our Theseus only.

For neither was it thunderbolts from Zeus
With flashing fire that slew him, nor the blast
Of whirlwind sweeping o'er the sea that hour,
But either some one whom the Gods had sent,
To guide his steps, or else the abyss of earth
In friendly mood had opened wide its jaws
Without one pang. And so the man was led
With nought to mourn for—did not leave the world
As worn with pain and sickness; but his end,
If any ever was, was wonderful.

*tr. by E.H. Plumtre*

Heraclitian harmony at the cosmic level is realized in *Oedipus at Colonus*. Oedipus, consumed in a blaze of light (a masculine symbol), issuing from a fissure in the earth (a feminine symbol), resolved, transcended the antagonistic forces of the psyche. By way of contrast, in *Oedipus Rex*, Oedipus' expiatory actions in blinding himself and going into exile are actions of a physically stressful, nontranscendent order. The almost unbearable tension resulting from the unresolved catastrophe, wherein all focus is on the tragic separation from ignorance and innocence, is not conducive to the harmony of Heraclitus. Rather, in this state of psychic tension, pity and fear, it might be proposed (Aristotle notwithstanding), are not purged; as Oedipus goes into exile, pity at his fate and fear for our own attend him. With *Oedipus at Colonus* materiality is transcended in a sublime psychic fusion effecting the hero's apotheosis. "The antagonism at the heart of the world," the psychic split between the tensional forces of suffering-restraint and joy-release, is resolved; the cosmic wound, incurred when matter and energy separated from original chaos, is healed.

Prevalent criticism adjudges *Oedipus at Colonus* a miracle play. Rather, it is here contended, *Oedipus at Colonus* is a cosmic tragedy, with transcendence, not deliverance of the individual, its objective. Neither Oedipus nor any tragic hero shares, as Eliade puts it, "religious man's profound nostalgia ...to inhabit a 'divine world'...a pure and holy cosmos, as it was

in the beginning, when it came fresh from the Creator's hands."
The tragic hero's profound nostalgia is to attain the beyond,
the chaos before creation, to transcend existence.

## IV. The Psychic Tragedy of Stress

The cosmic dimension achieved by Sophocles was denied to
Shakespeare, the dimensions of tragedy being defined by the
range of the philosophy of the creative artist. Although, with
Euripides, his vision projected far beyond the confines of
social and psychological humanism and though he touched the
farthest reaches of psychic experience, at the very brink of the
gulf separating psychic being from cosmic being-nonbeing he
stopped. His, and Euripides', was a dark philosophy. Its ultimate heroic action was one of separation.

The theme of the destruction of the ego, consciousness, the
will, is present in *Othello*; victim of the dark powers in his
nature, Othello surges to a self-annihilating close, alone in the
violence of his rage. Rooted in disruptive passion, *Othello* does
not effect a dialectic synthesis of psychic discord on a cosmic
level; rather, it freezes at the climactic rending in a laocoön-like
horror. The resolution, in which Othello falls, a dark shadow
on the light, upon Desdemona, completes an amorous emblem; the cosmic aspect is absent. Indeed, it never had been
present: the "chaos" of Othello's cry, III, iii, 90-91:

> But I do love thee! and when I love thee not,
> Chaos is come again.

refers to the state of intense distress he experiences upon
discovering (mistakenly?) the flawed nature of his love ideal.

*Hamlet* also remains on the psychic level. The stoically
inscrutable "The rest is silence" indicates passive dissolution of
the self; its tone, somber resignation. The dark irony which
informs the denouement is a far remove from the climactic
resolution in ecstasy of cosmic tragedy.

What Victorian moralist A.C. Bradley saw, in social terms, as an outcome of tragic waste in the serious works of Shakespeare, viewed from the perspective of the psychic tragedy of stress, is an outcome of psychic awareness, one fleeting instant of tragic insight into "the antagonism at the heart of the world," purchased at the cost of worldly existence. In the fall of Shakespeare's heroes we participate in an existential act of commitment that results in the hero's self-isolation.

The genius of Shakespeare is no less because of this cosmic limitation to his tragic action; the transcendent cosmic plane has (with the exception of late Sophocles, the German Romantic philosophers, particularly Schelling and Schlegl, the French Symbolists, such poets of personal mysticism as Blake and Yeats, and, in drama, Strindberg and Artaud) been a stranger to Western consciousness. Of Shakespeare's piercing awareness (if not consummated) of the cosmic dimension we have dramatic proof in *King Lear*.

The contradictions of the syncretic philosophies informing *King Lear* bar any certainty in its exegesis, yet it seems rather clear that the preachment of Christian submission in the Edgar-Gloucester subplot has no relevance to Lear's hideous world of monsters in the flesh. In Lear's descent there is discernible more than a trace of the Gnostic myth of the descent of Primal man into a world of demons, though the play, in its extreme pessimism, lacks the Gnostic faith in man's return from the depths and its attendant Oriental (especially Zoroastrian) concept that, in his rise, light is released from imprisoning matter-darkness. Lear's is a dark journey into the cold night, into a consciousness of the indifference of the universe and the inhumanity of man, a consciousness which freezes the blood. The gelid mystery behind existence is suggested in Cordelia's icy silence, a silence which a limited Western consciousness, blind to the state of non-being in original chaos, sees only as meaningless, having in Cordelia's words, "No cause." The subconscious, however, is not blind; in deep sleep Lear lies bound upon a burning wheel, emblematic of the passional friction resulting from the tormenting fragmentation of cosmic wholeness by the tyranny of time and matter. Awakening, and returning to the light of day, and to Cordelia, Lear returns to the world of temporal materiality. Submission, in his human frailty, to its dictates follows, a submission that lasts until his Fool (who has gone "to bed at noon," at the zenith of rational consciousness) is dead. Whereupon Lear returns to the subconscious level of intense revulsion at the feminine (a psychic eclipse described by the Chinese Book of Changes, *I Ching*: "When Yang has reached its greatest strengths, the dark power of Yin is born within its depths, for night begins at midday"), to a primitive horror at the monstrosity of the feminine principle, expressive of man's abhorrence of the disruption of primal chaos, and wholeness, by the separation of being from non-being, the structuring of the psychic field into masculine energy (light) and feminine matter (darkness). His final cry, in the context of this archetypal myth of creation, is one of horror: "Look on her, look, her lips,/ Look there, look there!"

So viewed, Cordelia is the sinister half of the Buddhist Yin-Yang symbol which Western man is unable, at least consciously, to accept, and toward whom he directs his feelings of guilt for the violation of unitary chaos by the original act of creation-destruction whereby emerged order, wave-form duality in the energic field, existence. As the oppositional element standing in the way of a realization of the transcendently formless form, "she" carries an incestuous attraction for Lear (as for all sentient men who carry "her" within) who yearns to possess "her," yet fears to be possessed by "her." Upon this wrack of the senses, upon this "burning wheel" of attraction and repulsion, Lear lies bound. The consummatory union of demon and demiurge leading to a reintegration of the psyche with the energic void beyond space and time, the return to the cosmic field is, in the dark Stoicism which pervades the catastrophe, denied to Lear. Thus viewed, *King Lear* is not a tragedy of cosmic transcendence but a tragedy of psychic stress.

## V. Visionaries of Cosmic Tragedy

After Shakespeare, through the seventeenth and eighteenth centuries, the imprint of transcendent motive upon drama is faint. With the coming of the Romantic movement, the outlines of the psychically projective-introjective cosmic impulse again took dramatic shape. Goethe, under its influence, absorbed the Eastern philosophic principle of the transcendent synthesis of opposing forces, and published his conception of it as "the demoniacal element" in personality. Of it Goethe wrote: "[It manifests] itself only in contradictions...[and] seems to step in between other principles...yet to unite them." In fire, the alchemical means to the transmutation of the elements, Goethe sought to transcend human existence: at the climax of *Egmont*, in a transcendent *auto-da-fé*, his hero is consumed in flames. Always driven by the desire to transcend matter—in his youth having attempted to transmute, through fire, gross stones into "virgin earth"—in his maturity Goethe felt compelled to proclaim the primal unity; as L.A. Willoughby has written: "For Goethe it was axiomatic that light, with its opposite pole, darkness, was the primal unity"; and, further, in a typically Romantic extravagance, to announce the religious oneness of East and West: "*Gottes ist der Orient! Gottes ist der Okzident!*" Goethe's intense conviction soon burned itself out and in his later writings he rejected the East.

What to Goethe had been but a brief flush of inspiration became to Strindberg an unflagging obsession. The fiery vision burned within him: during his *Inferno* period he strove, as had Goethe, to transmute matter in a fiery alchemical retort, to discover, figuratively, the Heaven of gold in the Hell of the diabolical element, sulphur. In his chemical experiments

Strindberg failed, but in his psychic "experiments," in his compulsive intuitional probings of his deeper self, Strindberg succeeded impressively. The fiery vision, which in *Egmont* provided a theatrically stirring finale, in Strindberg's *The Dream Play* became the climactic culmination of a complex pattern of symbolic action, action which pointed toward the transcendence of Western moral strictures in a Heraclitian fire. At the climax, Agnes (an early Christian martyr; also, "Agni," the Hindu deity of cosmic fire) enters the flaming tower, thereby, in this doubly significant symbol—the woman, in a mystic inversion of nature's order, entering into the male; both being consummed in flames—transcending the strifeful dualites of male-female, energy-matter, and truly realizing in dramatic form the synthesis of opposites of Vedic Hinduism, Heraclitus, and Nietzsche. In *The Dream Play* Strindberg attained Nietzsche's "hidden harmony in contrariety" as Cassirer phrased it—the power beyond good and evil.

Since Strindberg's lonely dramatic ventures into the ultimate of Eastern myth and philosophy, the "new" cosmos of psychic and parapsychic experience which Strindberg staked out for Western man has become a field of intensive psychological and anthropological research. The transcendental planes of myth and the deep strata of the subconscious, dream, and visionary image have been explored. Leading the way has been Carl Gustav Jung. "In dreams," Jung wrote in *Civilization in Transition*, "eternal man, dwelling in the darkness of primordial night,...[is] the whole, and the whole is in him." This mystic longing for wholeness, for the ultimate, has also been brought to Western attention by the influx of Eastern religions. Alan Watts reflects the transcendent Zen Buddhist goal of a simultaneous, yet beyond time, realization of the sublime state of being-nonbeing in describing, in *The Supreme Identity*, "the central drama...[as] the self-abandonment and self-realization of the ultimate and infinite."

In light of the prevailing interest in this fulfilling aspect of psychic experience—cosmic transcendence—a broadening trend is clearly evident, one which is enlarging Western awareness beyond its traditional bounds of consciousness. It seems reasonable to foresee cosmic consciousness exerting an ever greater influence on the philosophic cast of dramatic art. Bearing out this view, Karl Shapiro has written:

> It appears that in the twentieth century we have reached the point at which Oriental "ways of life" are about to penetrate the West. At the same time it appears that science has reached that frontier at which it meets up with what is called mysticism. We can see this in the reaction of Jung against Freud (cosmic versus rationalistic psychology), in the tremendous spurt of creative activity the world over, and in the speculations of cosmic scientists.... Cosmic consciousness is being forced upon the attention of the world from every side; the deep vein of mysticism has been opened again and the age of pure rationalism seems to be on the wane.... A tremendous synthesis is in the making between modern science, the ancient psychologies of the past, and what we call poetry or art.[1]

## VI. Summary

In summary, a distinction has been drawn between two levels of high tragedy: at the psychic level there is the psychic tragedy of stress, and at the cosmic level, the cosmic tragedy of transcendence. Noting the basic differences existing between Eastern and Western philosophies—the East: cosmically transcendent, conceiving the ultimate goal to be a unitary state beyond being and the tensional dualities of existence; and the West: psychically dualistic, with its ultimate goal a victory by the forces of light, energy, and the spirit, with a correlative defeat of the powers of darkness, matter, and the flesh—this

[1]"Poets of the Cosmic Consciousness," in *In Defense of Ignorance* (New York: Random House, 1952) p. 301.

chapter has recognized that tragedies of Eastern transcendence, being alien to the dominant rationalistic philosophies of the Western world, have been exceedingly rare. In fact, only *Oepidus at Colonus* and *The Dream Play* have been cited as dramatic realizations of the cosmic state of transcendence.

For over two millennia, Western drama, in the main, has been lacking in cosmic faith. Today there may be a surge of interest in Eastern insights (as noted above), but in terms of Western avant-garde drama there is little faith of any kind in man and still less faith in the meaningfulness of existence. Yet, as nature abhors a vacuum, so too man. Contemporary drama is a series of desperate attempts to escape the nihilistic void. Expressionist agony, surrealistic absurdity, existentialist commitment have provided slim ledges of refuge before the abyss of nothingness. For the many, in drama as in life, the rule has been survival of self at all costs, and the costs have been high. Still, in spite of this physiological maxim, nature is perverse and has not failed to produce, in this age as in all others, deviants from the norm. Two such recalcitrants are Antonin Artaud and the Albert Camus of *Caligula*.

As if in response to Artaud's frantic call for an atavistic release through a leap into a void (his Theatre of Cruelty), *Caligula* provides a vertiginous fall which so shocks reason as to destroy it. And in Caligula's awesome plunge is the demoniacal element of Goethe; in it we feel a marvelous triumph of vitalistic force over the passive void. With Othello, Caligula achieves a psychic triumph in defeat; yet a consummatory transcendence is not theirs at the climax. Rather, they attain the self-isolation of psychic tragedy. Caligula (last line, italics inserted): "*I* am alive!"

Conventional dramaturgical theory cannot explain this paradoxical effect of affirmation-in-destruction. Psychological studies, probing deeply into the oppositional complexities of psychic experience, have revealed the Aristotelian concept of the purging of the emotions (according to Nietzsche:

"pathological release") as plainly inadequate even to begin to explain the effects of psychic tragedy, much less cosmic tragedy. This ultimate level has been reached by Jungian aesthetic. Jung has recognized that man "lives" at a level beyond the emotions—in the spirit, a recognition shared by Nicolas Berdyaev: "Man's dissatisfaction with the finite, his longing for the infinite, reveals the divine in man." This spiritual element in each superior (heroic) man, "the sort of man who is only of any account," as Nietzsche has stated—each but a part of the psychic whole—yearns for the wholeness of its origin, and its destiny.

Dramatic theory, if it is to approach a comprehension of this mysterious compulsion to attain cosmic integration, or (falling short of integrative fulfillment) psychic separation, must move on the psychic-cosmic plane. At this level cosmic tragedy reveals the drama of transcendent return. In the wounding of the tragic hero, man is witness, and participant, in the mystic archetypal act which reconciles opposites; he sees, and senses, a wound which heals; through the agonistic passion is gained the transcendent apotheosis; through separation from the psychic self the psyche is made whole. In the act of violence inflicted upon himself man sees re-enacted the act of separation which violated the cosmic whole of original chaos. Cosmic tragedy, in this sublime immolation, plays a motile trace of passion into the rhythmically and cyclically structured field of our existence, into the transitory wave-form of inspiration and expiration, rise and fall, birth and death, which we shadow in the cloud chambers of our consciousness, and penetrates this shadow existence to the primal spark harbored at the center. Here, at the center, passion strikes flame—the all-engulfing Heraclitian fire. Part encompasses whole, point penetrates cosmic field, and the Heraclitian flux of becoming—the cyclic necessity, matter and energy—is transcended. We are one again with the primal chaos from whence we came and to which we shall return.

# The Emblems of "The Septem"

*The Septem*, the seven. In the culminating drama of Aeschylus' Theban trilogy, the number seven figures prominently. Whereas Sophocles closed his great trilogy upon the vanishment of Oedipus at Colonus, Aeschylus terminated his trilogy upon the expunging of the seven warriors and the two sons of Oedipus from the face of the earth. Whereas Sophocles narrowed his psychic locus to the fissure in the earth and the sky above Mount Cithaeron where Oedipus vanished, Aeschylus closed with the fatal engagement at the gates of Thebes and the trophy of destruction standing over the fallen pair.

This chapter proposes that Aeschylus' Theban trilogy, on the evidence of the surviving final drama, *The Septem*, is a profound psycho-mythic declaration of faith—the nature of such faith shall be the burden of this study to suggest. That the drama ends its dramatic conflict with "one," with the vertical column of destruction, is herein interpreted as having the deepest psychological and metaphysical significance.

Parenthetically, it should be remarked that the nature of Sophocles' culmination in naught, in an extinction—an "end, most wonderful"—of the existence in *Oedipus at Colonus*, has great consequence in terms of metaphysic and history: the non-Greek nature of this cancellation stirs a resonant chord, one sounded in India with the birth of Buddhism in the century preceding Greece's awakening—from a solitary bed of Homeric parthenogenesis the prevalent fashion in dramatic scholarship would have us believe.

The main points which shall be herein advanced will be found to center on Apollo, the Captain of Sevens. He is the force which destroys the seven and would destroy the city, and the defender who would preserve it. He destroys the men, but the city is, if only for a brief respite, preserved.

> CHORUS: Without a leader a city falls,
> As under a heavy curse. (764-65)[1]

Such is the political aspect of the trilogy.

But it is not its political aspects that probe psychic depths. Rather, these depths are revealed in the mythic valences of numerological symbology.

The numbers having psychic powers are seven and one. "Seven" has reference to the seven warriors and to Apollo, Captain of Sevens. "One" relates to the solution to the riddle of the Sphinx, the "one" of man, as Oedipus frames the answer, or, alternatively, the one of the god who oversees the action, Apollo. This, it is proposed, is borne out on the emblems of the shields.

The play ends in darkness. Yet through the darkness of night stands the trophy of destruction, a testimony to death, and one celebrating a firm faith in the ineluctable urge of society and its gods to return from darkness into the light.

---

[1] Citations are the author's.

We now proceed to essay an archetypal reading of the earliest extant drama of heroic and tragic confrontation.

*The Septem* presents a dramatic battle within the psyche of the tragic hero, Eteocles. At the point where opposing forces meet Apollo stands.

The god of order, Apollo symbolizes the divine syncretism of opposing forces. At Delphi he dwells with Dionysus. W.K.C. Guthrie has remarked upon the close mingling of the two gods in the Aeschylean fragment (341) which speaks of Apollo in Dionysiac terms: "the ivied, the Bacchic."[2]

Orgiastic release was Dionysus'. The "release" from the searing beam of Apollo's eye was in destruction, in drought and plague, a fact of which Eteocles was well aware:

> Phoebus rides the destroying wind
> That sweeps away hated Laius and his kin.
> (689-90)

"Seven" is a number that had mystic significance to Apollo: the seventh-month child who, on his birthdate, the seventh of Bysios, returns from his winter journey to resume his seat at the sacred *omphalos* of Delphi; the god who, from Zeus, received the seven pieces of Dionysus and set them beside his tripod; the god who mastered the seven-stringed lyre and by its harmonies guided Amphion in the laying of the stones that formed the wall of Thebes; the god who stands at the seventh gate over the fallen sons of Oedipus. As the Messenger informs us:

> Six gates stand;
> Apollo, at the seventh,
> Venges Laius' fatal flaw.
> (799-801)

---

[2] W.K.C. Guthrie, *The Greeks and Their Gods* (Boston: Beacon, 1950), p. 202.

It is in light of this high relevance of Apollo to the Oedipal trilogy that one might be led to examine his bearing on the inceptive riddle of the Sphinx. The action works out Apollo's dictate. Significance might well attach to correspondences between the sequence of the riddle—four, two, three, (one)—and myths involving Apollo.

We begin with "four." Four adamantine columns rose from the sea upon Leto's giving birth to Apollo on Delos in the Cyclades.

Next, "two." Two, the opposed duality beneath all that exists, might well refer to the opposition-and-resolution of these opposed forces in the syncretism of Apollo and Dionysus at Delphi.

"Three" is the number of coils made by the python which Apollo slew and which poised beneath his tripod. And three is the number of warnings given by his oracle to Laius. As "four" symbolizes birth, "three" symbolizes death, the death meted out by Apollo, the Far Darter. Birth (four), and death (three), making a total of seven; and between (two), a span of fated life for man who walks, two-footed, striding the earth in his pride at noontide, until by some mysterious gnosis he discerns his return to the delta, female symbol of the womb, at death and the coming of darkness.

Textual evidence that man is the centered figure in the Sphinx's riddle of existence—four, two, three—is to be found in the exceedingly intricate imagery Aeschylus employs in describing the emblems upon the shields of the Argive attackers. He has the Messenger close his account of the emblems with a challenge:

> These are the signs.
> (649)

A sign must be read. One reading, I propose, will find the emblems descriptive of the journey from darkness to light and back into darkness that defines the journey all existents must take.

The seven shields, essentially, fall into three groups. First, five violent warriors, suggestive of the five Spartoi who founded Thebes, earth-sprung from teeth of the dragon, serpent guardian of Ares' spring, the Northern god who executed Apollo's will. Second, the single figure of Amphiaraus, the seer who goes knowingly to his death. And third, Polyneices.

Elements of the descriptions of the five warriors' emblems bear on the second part of the Sphinx's riddle: "What walks on two feet at noon?"

> MESSENGER:
> Tydeus is in a fury at midday.
> > (380)

> Capaneus finds the lightning
> Like unto the sun's noontime fire.
> > (430-31)

> Upon Eteoclus' shield
> A storming warrior scales a ladder.
> > (465-66)

> Hippomedon in a circle
> Whirls his shield.
> > (489-90)

> Parthenopaeus, where Amphion lies,
> Stands at the North gate.
> > (526-27)

The fifth, at the North gate, has no direct solar referent, an absence which gains import when it is recalled Amphion suffered Apollo's wrath in the loss of his wife, Niobe, and their twelve children.

Of the third warrior who "scales a ladder," might this not symbolize the morning ascent of the sun?

Of the fourth, the whirl of the shield suggest Apollo's fatal discus which felled his companion, Hyakinthos.

Further reading of the emblems suggests the cyclic journey; the first shield bears

> At its center, on a field of stars
> A moon at the full.
> (388-89)

The moon, a symbol of Phoebe, sister of Themis, the first Delphic pythia; Phoebe who gifted Apollo with the seat of prophecy according to a myth attributed to Aeschylus;[3] Phoebe, identified with Phoebus Apollo by name, and by mythic action.

It bears note that the five warriors rose from earth (Themis-Pheobe), as does the sun, Apollo.

The two succeeding warriors symbolize the ascent of the burning disc, and the rise of hubristic man, Capanaeus bearing on his shield:

> ...a torch-bearing incendiary
> Who would set the city afire.
> (432-33)

The torch is the symbol of Ares, Apollo's executant of destruction.

Eteoclus, in the guise of a warrior who scales a ladder crying, "Not even the war god shall cast me down," (469) could be interpreted as a burning shadow of Eteocles, as Phoebe is the earthly shadow of Apollo, Phoebus Apollo.

With the fourth and fifth warriors we enter the descent phase

---

[3] T. Dempsey, *The Delphic Oracle* (London: Blackwell, 1918), p. 20.

of the solar round. Both bear signs of earthly power: Hippo-
medon's bears an image of

> Typhon belching smoke...
> (493)

and Parthenopaeus' carries "a devouring Sphinx." (541)

The Typhon was father of the Sphinx whose riddle suggests
the tragic fate: noontide *koros*, and eventide subsidence into
the telluric womb.

This mystic syncretism of sun and earth is found in the sixth
warrior, Amphiaraus. In his person Apollo and Themis are
fused. Upon his shield he bears no sign. Its brazen circle is as
clear as the face of the sun. But his inner sign, the divine psychic
self he as prophet possesses, reveals his symbolic significance.
The Messenger describes him:

> The harvest of his furrowed mind
> Is deep and rich.
> (593-94)

Here may be discerned reference to Themis, earth goddess of
prophecy and fertility, first occupant of Delphi's prophetic
seat.

Further, an allusion to Athena may well be present: she
sprang from the brow of Zeus, the furrowed brow. In the guise
of the sage, counselling prophet, Amphiaraus, she, the goddess
of ordered battalions, might be seen as here arrayed against
Ares, god of disordered ranks and battle rout.

But it is as the symbol of arcane wisdom, Themis, that the
shield and figure of Amphiaraus speak to the inner ear; hers is
the presence of divine intuitive wisdom, she the goddess of
divine justice.

On the shield of the seventh warrior, Polyneices, appears her
shadow:

> Justice leads the way.
> (644)

This may be seen to constitute a perversion of the original Delphic power, one which completes the cyclic pattern begun with the first shield whereon Phoebe, in a like perverse appropriation by the Argives, was pictured as a party to this unjust cause.

Origin and termination are earthly. The story in the shields portrays the wages of worldliness, the taint of materiality: from material substance to fire and return to matter—this the ascent and descent figured on the shields.

The deep irony which resides in the anagogic aspect of the symbolism of the shields deepens at the scene of threnodic despair wherein the Chorus cry over the vanquished sons of Oedipus:

> Beside the Gate stands
> The sign of destruction.
> (957-58)

And what is the nature of the "sign of destruction" which stands beside the seventh gate?

Might it not be Apollo, whose pillar protected city gates? The singular oneness of this Apollonian symbol marks a completion in unity of the sequence of the Sphinx's riddle: four, two, three, one. The four of birth; the two of man in his human pride; the three of the sacred tripod, standing above what has been, is, and is to be. And, finally, the one of the god who combines in his holy shrine at the Delphic navel stone and chasm the dual symbols of creation and destruction, of the god who raises over the victims of his far-darting arrow the trophy of destruction, testimony to death and the fated fall.

For all that rises must fall: man, his cities, and his golden god.

Such are the signs, of emergence and return, to be read in the shields of the fallen seven.

# The Most Subtle Geometry of John Webster in His "The Duchess of Malfi"
(with Anne Cinque)

Crown him a poet, whom nor Rome, nor Greece,
Transcend in all theirs for a masterpiece:
In which, whiles words and matter change...
he...to memory hath lent
A lasting fame, to raise his monument.

John Ford
                     Commendatory note to the Reader of
                     *The Duchess of Malfi*

Webster's borrowing has been the subject of extended study.

Webster's thought has not. Deplorably, most critics have seen *The Duchess of Malfi* to be little more than a ragged patchwork of aphorisms and sententiae, lacking in an informing moral vision.

Countering this critical write-off of Webster as thinker, we have (above) the firsthand view of John Ford, who advanced what might well be taken as the informing process that shaped *The Duchess of Malfi*: the meeting of contraries, mutability and constancy, and their transmutation, as in alchemy, into a *tertium quid* quite beyond categories.

Ford, with good cause, addressed "the Reader." In performance, subtleties are difficult to catch on the fly; only on reflection, in memory, does form emerge. It is almost as though Ford had in mind the audience of quick-studies at Blackfriars which Henry Fitzjeffries played pander to, some four years after the play's first performance, in penning his superficial caricature: "...crabbed (Websterio)/...It will be so obscure/ That none shall understand him (I am sure)."

Well, the play has been in print for some three and a half centuries and the obscurities which so vexed Fitzjeffries might, by now, one might expect, have been cleared up. Such does not appear to be the case.

Case in point—the superscription, a Latin tag from Horace (*Epistles*, I. 6), that has been traced to Dekker's moral tract *Lanthorne* (Lantern) *and Candle-light* (1609). But the significance Webster might have intended and how Dekker's work might bear upon *The Duchess* remain an inscrutable mystery. F.L. Lucas[1], found it "obscure in the extreme."

Yet Dekker, in context, makes its meaning abundantly clear.

Horace: If you know something better, impart it openly; if not, make use of these precepts.

Dekker (in closing his tract, before employing the Horatian tag):
...to him that embraceth his labours, he dedicates both them and his love: with him that either knows not how, or cares not to entertaine them, he will not be angry, but onely to Him sayes this much for a farrewell.

---

[1] *The Complete Works of John Webster*, ed. F.L. Lucas (London: Chatto & Windus, 1927).

In effect, Dekker says there's more here than meets the eye. Those who get it, fine; the rest? Farewell.

Webster, in eliding from Horace "something better," underlined this allusion to the presence of a deeper meaning in his work:

> If you know—[elision, implying "anything"]
> Impart it openly...
>          (Tr. Gwendolyn Hull)

Thomas Middleton, in his commendatory verse to *The Duchess*, made much the same point:

> To Tragedy:
> As light at the Thunderer's stroke from darkness springs,...
> To the poet, life she brings.

Light from darkness, as in revelation.

The light from darkness motif was attached by Dekker to his *Lanthorne and Candle-light*:

> or
> the Bell-Mans second Nights-walke
> In which
> He brings to light...

and to his first assay at moral edification the year previous to Lanthorne (1609):

> *The Belman of London*
> BRINGING TO LIGHT...

Though Dekker's works deal rather heavily with the exposure of vice, the way in which he closed *The Belman* is instructive, and anything but obvious:

> . . .so many infected bodies being to bee found in every
> corner of the land, whome no medicine can cure, but the physicke
> whiche he bestowes upon him at the Gallowes? Where I
> leave them as to the haven in which they must cast an-
> chor, if Dericks Cables do but hold, and unlesse
> they amend. Give thanks to the Belman
> of London, if either profits or plea-
> sure bee gained by this
> Discovery.

An inverted pyramid, poised over the pregnant word "Discovery." It is companion to the intricately structured antithesis
of Bosola's conceit at the final descent of the Cardinal:

> That thou, which stood'st like a huge pyramid
> Begun upon a large and ample base,
> Shalt end in a little point, a kind of nothing.
> (V, v, 76—79.)[2]

The deepening of meaning in Webster (and the incompara-
ble energy of his style) in turning this compositional conceit of
Dekker to his dramatic, and thematic, purpose is not an exceptional case. *The Duchess of Malfi* is as much a magic act as a
drama: almost every speech is a model in the art of bringing
thought and word together briskly, with flashing wit. It is
almost as though Hotspur drove Webster's quill: "crabbed,"
indeed!

In seeking to trace the springs of Webster's most subtle
intelligence, a reading of a minor (or so the literature would
seem to indicate) source suggests that if Webster scholars, and
admirers of the brilliant Lord Brooke, Fulke-Greville, ever get
together there are likely to be two outcomes: a) Webster might

---

[2] *The Duchess of Malfi*, ed. John Russell Brown (Cambridge: Harvard
University Press, 1964).

at last get his intellectual due, and b) Fulke-Greville might at last get a production! For *Mustapha* deserves a showing, and hearing; written and rewritten,[3] and circulated privately among his friends (though published in a pirated edition in 1609 by one Nathaniel Butter, none other than the publisher of Dekker's *The Belman*), *Mustapha* evidences remarkable correspondences with *The Duchess*: a thematic similarity, and a most unusual one, is the proposal that the law of succession be overthrown in establishing as heir the mother's issue (II, ii, 101).

> DELIO: ...establish this young, hopeful gentleman
> In's mother's right.
> (V, v, 112-13)

And in Fulke-Greville we find Webster's preoccupation with the art of chart-makers and stargazers, geometry:

TIME: Let man drawe his owne cursed Square,
Such crooked lines, as his fraile thoughts affect:
And like things that of nothing framed are,
Decline unto that centre of defect...
    (Third chorus, 73—78)

BOSOLA:—didst thou never study mathematics?
OLD LADY: What's that, sir?
BOSOLA: Why, to know the trick how to make a many lines
meet in one centre...
    (II, ii, 21-23)

In both Webster and Fulke-Greville, the metaphor of a malevolent mist:

---

[3] Warwick ms., 1604-ca. 1613.

CHORUS OF CONVERTS: Man...[hath] made Hell
...in that darck'ned Orbe, through mists
which vice creates...
    (Fourth chorus, 2, 7)

BOSOLA: ...life a general mist of error,
...death a hideous storm of terror.
    (IV, ii, 188-89)

In both, thought of a universal conflagration, and, contributing to the fall, a threefold listing of vices that closely parallel:

ROSSA: I will beare with me, in this Bodies dust,
What curse soever to the earth remaines.
I will beare with me Envie, Rage, Desire,
To set all Hearts, all Times, all Worlds on fire.
    (V, 113-16)

1st MADMAN: [I] shall set all the world on fire
upon an instant...
    (IV, ii, 74-75)

FERDINAND: Whether we fall by ambition, blood, or lust,
Like diamonds, we are cut with our own dust.
    (V, v, 72-73)

In yet another play of Fulke-Greville (*Alaham*, 1600), Medea-like, the Senecan heroine, under press of horror, finds her grasp on her identity slipping. A similar moment of metaphysical quandary occurs in *The Duchess*:

HALA: But what is this? Wake I, or doe I dreame?
If chang'd; with whom or into whom am I?
Doth Horror dazell sense, or multiply?
What world is this?
    (V, ii, 98-102)

DUCHESS: Who am I?
BOSOLA: Thou art a box of worm-seed...
DUCHESS: Am I not thy duchess?
    (IV, ii, 123-24, 134)

And, in both Fulke-Greville and Webster, the archetypal theme of woman's perfidy:

ALAHAM: Possesse againe the State, where you beganne:
The Woman you; 'Tis we deceive the Man.
Enter upon this large infernall wombe;
Repay your selves; this mould did make you all.
    (V, ii, 130-35)

BOSOLA: O this gloomy world!
In what a shadow, or deep pit of darkness,
Doth womanish and fearful mankind live!
    (V, v, 100-03)

Geoffrey Bullough, in his edition of the collected works of Fulke-Greville,[4] remarks upon the poet's dramas as being of "earthly errors against a background of eternity," written with a "magnificence...of dark rhetoric." The evaluation could as aptly apply to Webster.

The Websterian "magnificence" of Fulke-Greville culminated in his *Caelica* (pre-1610). In such passages as sonnet VII we find that mystic intensity and reach that led Bullough to characterize Fulke-Greville's major motive as a "cosmic obsession." *Caelica* is deserving of such accolades:

The World, that all containes, is ever moving,
The Starres, within their spheres for ever turned,
Nature (the Queene of Change) to change is loving,
And Forme to matter new, is still adjourned.

---

4 Baron Fulke-Greville Brooke, *Poems and Dramas*, ed. Geoffrey Bullough (New York; Oxford University Press, 1945).

Fortune our phantasie-God, to varie liketh,
Place is not bound to things within it placed,
The present time upon time passed striketh,
With Phoebus wandring course the earth is graced.

The Ayre still moves, and by it moving cleareth,
The Fire up ascends, and planets feedeth,
The Water passeth on, and all lets weareth,
The Earth stands still, yet change of changes breedeth;

Her plants, which Summer ripes, in Winter fade,
Each creature in unconstant mother lyeth,
Man made of earth, and for whom earth is made,
Still dying lives, and living ever dyeth;

   Onely like fate sweet Myra never varies
   Yet in her eyes the doome of all Change carries.

Thus Fulke-Greville; and Webster, at the close, in a coda of Mozartian loveliness, catches an echo of Greville's ode to mutability:

DELIO: ...These wretched eminent things
Leave no more fame behind 'em than should one
Fall in a frost, and leave his print in snow;
As soon as the sun shine, it ever melts,
Both form and matter...
      (V, v, 113-16)

In framing such refined conceits both Fulke-Greville and Webster (and Donne) excelled. And much on their minds, serving as subject for their abstract wit, was the terrestrial and celestial art then much in vogue, geometry:

Geometrie gives measure to the earth below...
Shee teacheth, how to lose nought in my bounds,
And I would learne with joy to lose them all...
  Fulke-Greville, "A Treatie of Humane Learning"


BOSOLA: ...a kind of geometry is [a soldier's]
last supportation...to hang in a pair of slings,
take his last swing in the world upon an honourable
pair of crutches...
  (I, i, 61, 64-65)


Bosola draws a fantastic diagram of the progress of man
lamed: crutches planted, the invalid swings forward until the
weight is borne once again upon the good foot. Schematized,
the figure describes a diamond. In substance, adamantine,
imperishable; in shape a schema of the twin cones of optic
inversion by which the living object is trapped within the
converging perspective of the lens—the diamond is for Webster a central symbol of the tension between the press of birth
and death, between becoming and being, and of the desire to
escape the stressful duality of existence.
  Indeed, the diamond is the subject of the Duchess's first
aphoristic figure:


DUCHESS:              Diamonds are of the most value
They say, that have pass'd through most jeweller's hands.
  (I, i, 299-300)


A bitter poignancy informs her *mot*, it giving rise, after
Ferdinand's gross insinuation and her desperate counter asser-
tion of her "virtue," to the Cardinal's vicious metaphor for
woman: a lopped diamond through which lubriciously courses
the incontinent sand:

FERDINAND: Whores, by that rule, are precious—
DUCHESS:                                        Will you hear me?
I'll never marry:—
CARDINAL:                                So most widows say:
But commonly that motion lasts no longer
Than the turning of an hour-glass—the funeral sermon
And it, end both together.
    (I, i, 301-04)

The diamond, flawless collector of light, is clouded here with the dross of carnality. Later, as death approaches, Webster effects a dramatic change on the figure of diamond as symbol of light: then, in an ingenious and fantastical allusion to earth and sky as dual traps (a figure reminiscent of Fulke-Greville's *Mustapha*: "The earth draws one way, the skie another" [IV, i, 38]) the hour-glass becomes a Life-glass giving perspectives on perdition or redemption:

DUCHESS: I know death hath ten thousand several doors
For men to take their exits, and 'tis found
They go on such strange geometrical hinges.
You may open them both ways:—
    (IV, ii, 219-22)

Truly a remarkable conceit!—though written off in commentary as a mere "Senecan commonplace." Yet, in Seneca (*Epistles*, 70. 14), a colorless "*exitus multos*" is transformed with a flourish into "ten thousand several." Might this be yet one more instance of Webster's penchant for "borrowing" and then improving upon his source? Indeed it might—and from a most unlikely source, if Webster as rude assembler be credited. The possible source—Giordano Bruno, in his visionary *On the Infinite Universe and Worlds* (London, 1584): "not...one earth ...but ten hundred thousand...infinite globes..."

Yet, on reflection, is it so remarkable to find a connection between Webster and the mystic philosopher who was a guest of Fulke-Greville in 1584, which led to Bruno's *Ash-Wednesday Supper*, a Platonic dialogue on Copernican theory, having as its first section a dark journey by ferry and on foot, knee-deep in mud, "engulfed in a slimy passage," to Fulke-Greville's house near Charing Cross, in what can be seen as an Oedipal descent, and ascent—arriving finally "at a pyramid near the mansion where three streets meet," followed by an ethereal disquisition on the celestial spheres? And, further, is there not an echo of Bruno (and of the "dark philosopher," Heraclitus, celebrator of universal flux, whose "Night-walkers," in one of his more gnomic fragments [Fr. 78], would bathe in mire that their defilement might be purified) in Ferdinand's self-revelatory admission?

> FERDINAND: He that can compass me, and know my drifts,
> May say he hath put a girdle 'bout the world
> And sounded all her quicksands.
>     (III, i, 84-86)

The liquid, unstable—a dark chaos opposed to the formal order of a silver fountain—on such a symbol of lucent order Webster chose to open his drama:

> ANTONIO:                    I admire it [the French court]
> ...a fix'd order...
> Consid'ring duly, that a prince's court
> Is like a common fountain, whence should flow
> Pure silver drops in general...
>     (I, i, 4, 11-14)

The thought is close to that of Bruno in *Gli eroici furori*[5] in its search for a unifying light in a world of darkness  As Webster begins with a fountain of unity, so also Bruno: "...the

---

[5] *The Heroic Frenzies*, tr. Paul Eugene Memmo, Jr. (Chapel Hill: University of North Carolina Press, 1964).

light of Amphitrite...diffused through all; it is the fountain of unity..."—of Amphritrite, goddess of the shining sea.

Bruno, as did Webster, sought the mystic grace Fulke-Greville saw his dear friend attain in death (*Life of Sidney*): "...and in this...orb of contemplation he blessedly went on, with a circular motion, to the end of all flesh." Thus it was to mark an affinity of spirit that Bruno should have dedicated his heroically aspiring discourse to Sir Philip.

That Webster identified the French court with a fount of symmetry is also Brunian: before visiting London, Bruno had dedicated his *De umbris idearum* (On the Shadow of Ideas, Paris, 1582) to King Henri III of France, it being his first treatment of the Art of Memory.

Anent "memory," and the Memory Theaters of London's occult master, Robert Fludd, and the guest of London, Giordano Bruno, no dramatic poet ever displayed a greater mastery of the emblematic scenes and rhetorical figures these mnemonic processes sought to evince than John Webster. While little is known of his life, such is the breadth of his knowledge, one might justifiably imagine that he was an adept in the copious occult literature of the Renaissance. Opening on the unity of a silver fountain, Webster closes on the unity of the emblem of triumph, the crown. His thought bears a Brunian cast:

DELIO: Integrity of life is fame's best friend,
Which nobly, beyond death, shall crown the end.

...the beauty which is...unity itself,
entity and identity.
     Bruno, *Eroica furori* (255)

Integrity of character, transcending worldly confines, this is the end toward which Webster has been driving his action; the closing couplet marks his capping tribute to the star-girt lady of sorrow, And, as we are about to meet her for the first time, no Petrarchan lover could gentler be in framing her trim entry:

> ANTONIO: I'll case the picture up:—only this much—
> All her particular worth grows to this sum:
> She stains the time past, lights the time to come.
>          (I, i, 207-09)

Such is the beauty with which Webster infused *The Duchess of Malfi* that it appears he did not so much write a play as fashion a firmament. As in a star chart, the density of fiery points constellates about metaphoric centers, the profusion of figures being integrated into the overarching design, furnishing, as John Russell Brown has noted (in the Revels edition), "necessary 'fixes' " in charting the profound reaches of Webster's coruscating dark.

A star "fix": the metaphor is apt. The navigator's fix upon the wheeling stars is just such an operation as astrologians performed in seeking to form a schema of the astral forces bearing on life's course, as led Antonio to cast a horoscope for his newborn son: "being combust in the ascendant, signifies short life...a violent death..." (II, iii, 61, 63).

This astrolgic cast of the time of the drama, 1513, was, in the Jacobean period, confronted by the challenge of the New Science. Ever oblique in his approach, Webster has the Cardinal, in his exchange of bawdry with Julia, slyly allude, by way of the dichotomous "fixed" and wandering stars of astronomy (and, as well, the "fixed" and volatile elements of alchemy-chemistry), to the biological dichotomy; man—constant, woman—fickle:

> CARDINAL:                                    You fear
> My constancy, because you have approv'd
> Those giddy and wild turnings in yourself.
> JULIA: Did you e'er find them?

CARDINAL:                         Sooth, generally for women:
A man might strive to make glass malleable,
Ere he should make them fixed.
JULIA:                                            So, my lord—
CARDINAL: We had need go borrow that fantastic glass
Invented by Galileo the Florentine,
To view another Spacious world i'th'moon
And look to find a constant woman there.
  (II, iv, 10-18)

"A constant woman...": beneath the surface ribaldry, a sober intent, the equivoque of the Cardinal and his jade masking the poignant referent, the perdurable symbol of constancy, the Duchess. For Webster's is a divine geometry, far transcending the arch thrusts of the Cardinal, and the earthbound diagrams Bosola and Ferdinand would draw on the night sky:

BOSOLA:                                          ...i'th'stars.
FERDINAND:                                    Why some
Hold opinion, all things are written there.
BOSOLA: Yes, if we could find spectacles to read them—
  (III, i, 59-61)

Yet, such is the mystic turning of Webster's dark world, this knavish twosome, this sullied pair, Fortune's chattels, are to be graced with a lifting of the veil and a blinding vision that gives rise to a moment of transport such as no drama has ever excelled:

BOSOLA: Fix your eye here:—
FERDINAND:                                    Constantly.
BOSOLA:                                         Do you not weep?
Other sins only speak; murder shrieks out:
The element of water moistens the earth,
But blood flies upward, and bedews the heavens.
FERDINAND: Cover her face: mine eyes dazzle: she died young.
  (IV, ii, 258-64)

Uncited in the critical tracing of sources for this divine stroke
is a work which, as noted, had been published in London
(1585), dedicated to Sir Philip Sidney, and bearing the author's
emblem, "the wheel of fixed time moving about its own
center"—Bruno's *Eroica furori* (72, 243):

> The [lover, the *third* of nine] blinded by the
> sudden...intense light, [a] celestial beauty
> ...emerging from the darkness...dazzles him.

Bruno offers an exegesis of the triadic significance: "Venus,
goddess of the third sphere" (167), and Apollo (264), instinct
and intellect conjoined, the mystic *coniunctio,* the *coincidentia
oppositorum* of alchemy, and, as divine alkahest, a moral beauty.

That Webster knew Bruno's abstruse philosophic work, the
intricate order of his tragedy would suggest. Yet the striking
figure of a lover blinded might have reached him by way of a
ballad (anonymously written and printed before 1603 in the
Shirburn collection), though in a context so far removed from
the ecstatic transfiguration of Webster—a maid's coy rejection
of a shepherd's armorous suit—as to make such a borrowing
most unlikely:

> Thy glorious beauty's gleam dazzles my eyesight,
> Like the sun's brightest beam shining at midnight.
>     "Phyllida Flouts Me"

No, we are not in a meadow radiant in the night, but in a
formal garden, within a symmetry, strict and perfect. With the
death of the Duchess, the declination into the carnage of the
final act commences; we shall descend, but the light of this
orient scene will not fade. The lovely figure with which Antonio opened, the fountain "whence should flow/Pure silver
drops..." has, as by alchemy, been transmuted into the reful-
gent countenance. The final act, such is Webster's subtle

genius, is to be a dark field for the Glory that persists in vision, as in the tender moment when, as the plaint of her echo reaches us, we sense in the shadow the light of her imperishable presence:

> ANTONIO: I mark'd not one repetition of the echo
> But that: and on the sudden, a clear light
> Presented me a face folded in sorrow.
>    (V, iii, 43-45)

Nietzsche remarked on the negative disc which the sun imprinted on the eye as an after image; Webster effected a mystic inversion of this optic priniciple. His play is no tragedy of blood; rather, it is a play of the spirit, a mystery of light.

It is no accident that *The Duchess of Malfi* opens, in contrast to the opening of *The White Devil*, "Banish't!" with "You are welcome to your country, dear Antonio..." in the person of Delio. In his constancy, he is a reflection of the radiant Duchess, a social ground to her metaphysical light. It is Delio who, Creon-like, after the tragic sacrifice (by death of banishment), contributes to the succession. Indeed, his seeking at the close "To establish this young, hopeful gentleman/In's mother's right" (V, v, 112-13) has a Eumenidean ring. And this after the Furies of the final act had visited the "Death, and disease through the whole land," as framed in Antonio's oracular premonition (I, i, 15)

While it may be only adventitious that a connection exists between "Delio" and "Delos," the latter the birthplace of Apollo in the Cyclades, at the center of a circle of islands and the flashing silver of his ringing court of porpoises, and while, admittedly, Webster merely took the name "Delio' from Bandello's tale (though the name had special meaning to the author, he having signed many of his love sonnets "Delio"), a further connection that seems more than coincidental merits mention: in Athens (as in Malfi) a plague was lifted by resort to a mystic geometry—the oracle at Delos having challenged the Athenian geometers to solve "the Quadrature," the famous conundrum of the-squaring-of-the-circle, also known as "the Delian Problem." A square and a circle? This might, on first glance, not seem to relate to the dominant geometric imagery in the play; but a square, poised on its corner, becomes a diamond.

A diamond within a circle, these the emblematic elements of Webster's mystic geometry: the circle, symbol of wholeness and of containment; of time's moving wheel and the stillness of the center, which, joined to the diamond, takes shape as the spinning top.

In this complex crystal wherein refract antinomies, Heraclitian and Parmenidean, we find the key to the declination-ascension and the all-cancelling stasis of Webster's most subtle geometry of fire and dark.

The circle, symbol of wholeness, and of containment:

DUCHESS:                                    ...here upon your lips
I sign your *Quietus est*:—                 [*Kisses him.*]
...All discord, without this circumference...
    (I, i, 463-64, 469)

The circle, obversely, symbol of containment, and of wholeness:

DUCHESS:                              Fie, fie, what's all this?
One of your eyes is blood-shot—use my ring to't
...my wedding ring,/...to help your eyesight.
ANTONIO: You have made me stark blind.
    (I, i, 403-05, 409-10)

Love...opens dark portals of diamond.
    Bruno, *Eroica furori* (93)

The diamond within a circle: symbol of mutability, and of transcendence:

DUCHESS: I have seen my little boy oft scourge his top
And compar'd myself to't: naught made me e'er
Go right but heaven's scourge-stick.
    (III, v, 79-81)

The Duchess, driven, scourged, spinning, her "life...a top which whipping sorrow driveth..." The metaphor is after Fulke-Greville's *Caelica* and Sidney: "a top which nought but whipping moves.../ The kindly way to beat us to our blisse" (*Arcadia*, II, xii).

Thus, a conventional, if striking, conceit. Yet, in its context, it is a metaphor bearing deep meaning; for a top is a diamond which, spinning, "sleeps," a paradox: circumferential swirl, about a still center of immutable tranquillity:

DUCHESS:  I am Duchess of Malfi still.
...[*Kneels.*] Come violent death,
Serve for mandragora to make me sleep!
    (IV, ii, 142, 234-35)

CARIOLA: What think you of, madam?
DUCHESS:                                   Of nothing:
When I muse thus, I sleep.
    (IV, ii, 14-15)

A sleep of sweet oblivion:

ANTONIO:                                   Do not weep:
Heaven fashion'd us of nothing, and we strive
To bring ourselves to nothing:—
    (III, v, 82-83)

A journey begun in the moving stillness of the center, at the lovers' troth:

ANTONIO: And may our sweet affections, like the spheres,
Be still in motion.
   (I, i, 481-82)

A journey ending in the stillness of death:

BOSOLA:                    I am the common bellman
...sent to condemn'd persons
The night before they suffer:—...
                           Hark, now everything is still.
   (IV, ii, 173-178)

Or so her tormentor, "the Belman," would have her believe.

Yet a truer tracing of the geometry of the spirit he had made for the Duchess in his own person. Despite his role of clever intriguer, Bosola spoke true:

DUCHESS:                   I could curse the stars.
BOSOLA:                        O fearful!
DUCHESS: ...may the world
To its first chaos.
BOSOLA: Look you, the stars shine still:—
   (IV, i, 96-98)

"Still": the motionless array descried in the night sky which physician to the Queen, William Gilbert (*On the Magnet*, 1600), apostrophized:

> How immeasurable...must be the space which
> stretches to those remotest of fixed stars!...
> There can be no movement of infinity and of an
> infinite body...

Yet the notes to the play prepared by Lucas and Brown,[6]

---

[6] Lucas in his edition of *The Complete Works* and Brown in his edition of *The Duchess*.

observing that "still" means, merely, "always, continuously,"
have not taken into account the rhetorical wordplay, delight-
ing in ambiguity, which so marked this age of Metaphysical
wit. A safe rule to follow with Webster: nothing is as it appears
on the surface; look beneath, or beyond.

Indeed, at the outcry of the bereft Ferdinand, poised, in his
grief, on the brink of madness:

> Did any ceremonial form of law
> Doom her to not-being?
>     (IV, ii, 300-01)

there is reason to give an obverse reading to his distraught
consignment of his sister to a doomed state, Bruno (in *Eroica
furori*, 222) having defined "*non*-being" as "subject to motion."

The death of the Duchess was triumphant; the serenity of her
spirit as she submitted to her executioners transformed an act
of horror into one of sublime tragic exaltation. In death, she
revealed an inviolable "Integrity."

That Giordano Bruno should be a source for this triumph of
the spirit is just: it had been little more than a decade since he,
much akin to the Duchess, had been cruelly executed, a victim
of the Inquisition, bound to a fiery stake in the Eternal City,
from whence his triumphal spirit ascended above The Field of
Flowers. Can we smugly assume that Webster was unaware of
the contemporaneous "mist of error... hideous storm of terror"
then sweeping the land of Machiavelli and of Dante, as they
had the century before in such actions of human savagery and
magnificence as to stir a fire within the poet one would have to
scale Olympus to find an equal of?

Webster, aware of the dawning New Science of "Galileo the
Florentine," does not celebrate it as an advance for man.
Rather, with his King, he would recognize the claims of the
dark past, of Bruno's enigmatic Seals, of the emblematic books

whose mottoes and glosses so closely parallel his dramatic practice, and the Theaters of Memory of Bruno and Fludd.[7]

The hermetic emblem of The Duchess which, for us, is most vividly inscribed on memory is, as noted, a diamond within a circle. It stands, not coincidentally we would suggest, as the mystic seal of "The Heaven" in Bruno's *The Art of Memory*, *Thirty Seals* (and the Key to the Seal of Seals) (London, 1583).[8]

Within the circle, at the center of the four radiating arms of the cross within the diamond, in an echo of the silver fountain which graced the beginning of our journey—its four arms issuing from the center as the four rivers flowing from the Tree of Paradise—the Duchess found the way to the stillness of the center.

Much as in the mystic vision of Rabbi Joseph ben Shalom (Barcelona, 13th century) who saw an abyss of nothingness in each earthly pang and in the poetry of another valiant solitary. Emily Dickinson (512, 650).

The Soul has Bandaged moments—[9]

Pain—has an Element an Element of Blank—[10]

the Duchess attains tragic release in a poignant blotting out of being.

And, as well, the tragic (Euripidean) hero, Bosola, who, with his Duchess (IV, ii, 155, 156), "most ambitiously" would "grow fantastical in our death bed."

---

[7] Frances A. Yates, *The Art of Memory* (Chicago: University of Chicago Press, 1966).

[8] Ibid.

[9] *The Complete Works of Emily Dickinson*. ed. Thomas H. Johnson (Boston: Little, Brown and Company, 1st ed., 1960). p. 512.

[10] Ibid., p. 650.

BOSOLA: ...Mine is another voyage. [*Dies.*]

What Webster with the magic spectacles of genius read in the Jacobean dark at the point of vanishment was a prevision of an insight of Newton in *Opticks*: at the plane of focus is the point of inversion: at the vanishing point, value inverts.

It is the vision of Nietzsche:

Self-knower!
Self-executioner!
Crammed between two nothings...

It is the vision of Webster—Self-transcender!

His Duchess is Sophia.

Uncover her face, and discover
"the dazzled Soul."[11]

---

[11] Ibid., p. 393.

# The Strange Pedantry of William Rowley in "The Changeling"

The fate of *The Changeling* at the hands of contemporary critics is a source of puzzlement.

The new criticism has come and gone; yet as far as *The Changeling* is concerned it might just as well have never existed. Oddly, there has been little, if any, close criticism of the text. Two BBC productions blithely dropped the subplot, and no one seems to have been upset at the omission. Apparently the main plot's love-intrigue between Beatrice and De Flores has been all the critical fraternity appreciate; indeed, enough to move them to acclaim its greatness:

> *The Changeling* has always...been accorded the first place among Middleton's serious works, and a very high position in the whole body of Elizabethan tragedy.[1]

---

[1] Samuel Schoenbaum, *Middleton's Tragedies, a Critical Study* (New York: Columbia University Press, 1955).

> In some respects in which Elizabethan tragedy can
> be compared to French or Greek tragedy, *The
> Changeling* stands above every tragic play of its
> time, except those of Shakespeare.[2]

Granted.

But, getting back to that troubling puzzlement, is this suffi-
cient acclaim? Why this reservation "except for Shakespeare"?
And is this acclaim fairly apportioned? What credit is due its
collaborator, William Rowley?

Briefly, I propose that *The Changeling*

> 1) stands above Shakespeare in the complexity and
> depth of its thought with respect to the carnal pas-
> sions, and
> 2) rises to this eminence through the genius of the
> almost universally abused William Rowley.

I will not pursue the first point. Let Shakespearean scholars,
if they wish, challenge it, and well and good if they do. It is time
*The Changeling* received close study. On the second, I said
"almost universally abused William Rowley" with the one
exception to the critical write-off of Rowley in mind, that of
Arthur Symons in *The Cambridge History of English Literature*.[3] It is hard to believe this lone voice sounded in Edwardian
times, and harder to feature that it had no echoes in a supposedly more sophisticated age concerning the very matters of
sexual psychopathology which, when he found them in *The
Changeling*, moved Symons to grant his unusual kudo to
Rowley:

---

[2] T.S. Eliot, *Selected Essays* (New York: Harcourt, 1932).

[3] Arthur Symons in *The Cambridge History of English Literature*, VI,
eds. Sir A.W. Ward and A.R. Waller (Cambridge: Cambridge University
Press, 1932).

>...the influence of Rowley upon Middleton
>[created]...a new capacity for the
>rendering of great passions and a loftiness
>in good and evil which is not to be recognized
>as an element in Middleton's brilliant and
>showy genius.

Symons, for all his amazingly progressive tolerance for the tragic passions, was a prisoner of his time when it came to morals. He let morality cloud his aesthetic judgment, speaking of "the nobility of even what is evil in the passions." But perhaps there is little cause to fault him when we take a look at the fire-and-brimstone fundamentalism of criticism in the Fifties and Sixties.

Samuel Schoenbaum finds "the dramatist," Middleton, of course (Rowley, being "a third-rate dramatist," is beneath notice), "preoccupied with sin and deterioration" of "sexually obsessed and morally perverse figures." N.W. Bawcutt in his edition of the play[4] describes it in similar terms as "a study in sin and retribution," while R.J. Kaufmann[5] sees it as dealing in "degenerate appetites." No hint here of that Symonian "loftiness in...evil." And it is just this paradox, the elevation in descent, that is the change at the heart of *The Changeling*. Or so it shall be the burden of this chapter to prove by reference to the text.

But first, and to get another, if related, matter of no little consequence to me out into the open, a brief side-glance at the question of just-who-wrote-what, and, more particularly, what significance the subplot might have in relation to the central theme of carnality triumphant.

As to who-wrote-what, we happily have all critics agreeing,

---

[4] *The Duchess of Malfi*, ed. N.W. Bawcutt (Cambridge: Harvard University Press, 1958).

[5] R.J. Kaufmann, *Elizabethan Drama, Modern Essays in Criticism* (New York: Oxford University Press, 1961).

after Frederick Gard Fleay,[6] that Middleton worked out the love-intrigue between Beatrice and De Flores in all but the opening and closing. Rowley wrote the first act, getting the action underway, and none too well, if one credits the view advanced by Richard Hindry Barker:[7] "The murder story is set in motion by Rowley, who tells it in the amiable, vulgar, and conventional way that is so very characteristic of him." Rowley also wrote the final scene in which Beatrice and De Flores "get theirs" for their sins, or so a morally oriented reading might presume. And Rowley wrote the subplot: the "silly subplot,"[8] the "trashy comic subplot,"[9] "sadly marred...by the lunatic divertissements,"[10] the "vehicle for clowning."[11] And, adding to the chorus of critical dismissal, Robert R. Reed: "If...Middleton's great tragedy succeeded, it has done so in spite of its mad scenes."[12] Finally, Samuel Schoenbaum gives the old heave-ho to "third-rate" Rowley, deeming his approach to be "essentially nonpsychological."

Well, this is too much. The play is a penetration into psychic change, and said penetration is made by one William Rowley. How wrongheaded the critics, and none more so than R.J. Kaufmann, who has the idea straight, but not its source: "The play could well be called *Middleton's Metamorphoses*." Row-

---

[6] Frederick Gard Fleay, *A Biographical Chronicle of the English Drama, 1559-1642* (London: Reeves & Turner, 1891).

[7] Richard Hindry Barker, *Thomas Middleton* (New York: Columbia University Press, 1958).

[8] E.H.C. Oliphant, *Shakespeare and His Fellow Dramatists* (New York: Prentice-Hall, 1929).

[9] J.S.P. Tatlock and R.G. Martin, eds., *Representative English Plays* (New York: Appleton-Century, 1938).

[10] Hazleton Spencer, ed., *Elizabethan Plays* (Boston: D.C. Heath, 1933).

[11] Patricia Thomson, *Sir Thomas Wyatt and His Background* (Stanford: Stanford University Press, 1964).

[12] Robert R. Reed, *Bedlam on the Jacobean Stage* (Cambridge: Harvard University Press, 1952).

ley's rather. For who but Rowley effected the changes in Beatrice-Joanna? Did he not plot the opening scene where, but five days after her acquaintance with Piracquo, her betrothed, she finds her womanly nature shifting to another swain, Alsemero?

> BEATRICE: [*aside*] I shall change my saint,
> I fear me; I find
> A giddy turning in me.

And who but Rowley worked the final changes in this inconstant daughter of Eve (V, iii), her sudden shift from a hardened and a hypocritical adultress who would confess to murder to protect her honor into a most contrite supplicant? For this, I suggest, is the awful change: her betrayal of her blood, hers the plunge from the loftiness of "evil" passion to the abysm of guilt and remorse.

And in illuminating, as it were, Beatrice's "fall" from "sinning" grace, Rowley has designed an unbelievably intricate mystic pattern. I know of none that equals it in subtlety and profundity. And once again I find that Arthur Symons sensed this secret: Rowley, Symons wrote some seventy years ago, "will set consciences or clowns arguing in terms of strange pedantry." Symons clearly had in mind the much-maligned subplot.

And, in venturing down this dark corridor of magic transformations of which, seemingly, Jacobean scholars of the drama have no inkling, where better to begin than with one "silly" exchange in I, ii between the antic Lollio and his master, the cuckold doctor, who are to oversee the mad scenes that perform a function extending far beyond the anti-masque parody of the main action which William Empson in "Some Versions of Pastoral"[13] would grant them. Here, in this first encounter with the Bedlamites we have an instance of the

---

[13] William Empson, *English Pastoral Poetry* (New York: Norton, 1938).

sinister arts Rowley manipulated so dextrously. Here we find allusions to astrology which the wits of the playhouse would have readily identified and delighted in. It is to be a basis on which the sequent action Middleton treated in V is to be worked out. The passage—Lollio's assignment of body parts to the hours (I, ii). It involves a conventional ordering of experience which Rowley could be sure the sixteen editions (1600-1618) of it source, *The Kalendar of Shepherds*, would have made familiar to his audience.

Lollio ticks off the seven hours and their associated body parts, equatable to the seven planets. While we shall have reason to examine them in detail when we come to consider the equivalent action in V, for the present, in seeking to point what strikes me as the central theme and Rowley's attitude toward it—his cynical amusement at the sexual core of rude existence, the mutability of erotic feeling, its shocking of opposites, visual and visceral, in the love/lust act—it is necessary that we only consider its inceptive and culminating actions.

> LOLLIO: ...for every part has his hour:
> we wake at six and look about us, that's eye-hour;
> ...at twelve go to dinner, that's belly-hour.
> ALIBIUS: Profoundly, Lollio! It will be long
> Ere all thy scholars learn this lesson...

Then, as if to stress this psychological verity underlying the love-feast, Rowley returns at the closing lines of I to this master metaphor of carnal appetite:

> ANTONIO: I would see the madmen....
> They bite when they are at dinner, do they not, coz?
> LOLLIO: They bite at dinner, indeed, Tony,
> Well I hope to get credit by thee; I like thee best;
> of all the scholars that ever I brought up...

The fineness of Rowley's hand in structuring the action to

carry out this master figure of shocked psychic change in the love intrigue from optic to peptic satisfactions roughened in the design of the contrast between the play's opening and close. The opening line discovers Beatrice in a whited sepulchre: " 'Twas in the temple where I first beheld her." Toward the close, De Flores, emerging from the closet with Beatrice stabbed, her life's blood quickly letting, exclaims upon her, and his own, figurative embowelment in the black demesne: "Now we are left in hell," to which Vermandero responds, extending the figure: "We are all there; it circumscribes here." Such an obvious contrast explains the religious perspective discerned by many critics. It may thus be seen as, ostensibly, a movement from innocence to damnation. Yet within the opening scene Rowley gives to Vermandero, Beatrice's father, lines hinting at a deeper mystery:

> VERMANDERO: ...our citadels
> Are plac'd conspicuous to outward view,
> On promonts tops, but within are secrets.

We are to hear more of "secrets" in the subplot action of III wherein Antonio, "the Changeling," gives proof of the occult scholarship Lollio (I, ii) saw him possessing:

> ANTONIO: Love has an intellect...
> ...brings all home into one mystery,
> Into one secret.

The "secret" of the duality of attraction-rejection in the erotic is given yet another expression—satisfaction-revulsion— by Rowley in the very opening. Alsemero intuits this bifurcation at the root of desire: "There's scarce a thing is both lov'd and loath'd...." The shift between is most subtle. We are to see that psychic inversion in Beatrice, "the changeling," the inconstant woman, in her shift from professed contempt for the reptilian De Flores to an active admiration for and complicity in his cunning; she, as she herself remarks, is to "stroke a serpent" (V, iii).

For it is woman, we see, who changes; man, the agent who effects her change. The inversion of sex roles in paradise myth is evident.

Yet the change is a product of the false report of our eyes. We "see" Beatrice's "change" with the eyes of "intellectual judgment," and see falsely. She only seemingly changes if we credit the infatuate descriptions of her two suitors: Alsemero who would set her in a holy temple; Piracquo who would be an enemy to any "that should but think she knew the meaning of inconstancy." In actuality, hers is the Cressid part, fickle to the core. De Flores, in II, bespeaks the masculine cynicism toward "that broken rib of mankind" in Middleton's manly directness of phrase:

> DE FLORES: ...if a woman
> Fly from a point, from him she makes a husband,
> She spreads and mounts then like arithmetic,
> One, ten, a hundred, a thousand, ten thousand....

De Flores knows her secret lust and tells her so: " 'Twas chang'ed from thy first love, and that's a kind / Of whoredom in thy heart..." (III, iv).

The "secret" of distaff inconstancy is open knowledge in the patrician society: woman is not to be trusted. Even the noble Alsemero must test his bride-to-be to ensure that she is virginal. He would avail himself of "a pretty secret / By a Chaldean taught me" (IV, ii) which he learned in *The Book of Experiment, called Secrets in Nature.*

Mention of Chaldean mysticism introduces overtly the bases for the philosophy of change which is the key to understanding the process of psychic change in *The Changeling.* The Chaldeans were, then as now, revered in occult circles as the source of transformational arcana. Rowley and Middleton (for theirs is a close collaboration in the framing of the mystically based symbolism that infuses the action of both underplot and main plot) in structuring metaphors of inversion employ three mystic Chaldean "sciences": numerology, astrology, and alchemy.

It may tax the patience of a modern audience to delve, as delve one must if one is to do justice to the "strange pedantry" of Rowley (and Middleton), into this abstruse lore, yet not overtax it: certainly the process is not unfamiliar to the follower of Jungian approaches to literature. So, without further caveat, we begin at the most difficult, the numerological allusions to an inversion of a Christian mystery in the seeming prattle of Tony, the self-professed changeling.

In III, iii, in the scene directly after De Flores' murder of Piracquo at Beatrice's behest, Rowley has Lollio and Antonio engage in inversionary word-play:

> LOLLIO: How many is one hundred and seven?
> ANTONIO: One hundred and seven is seven hundred
> and one, cousin.
> LOLLIO: This is no wit to speak on!

The train of allusion readable in this exchange is admittedly slender, yet it may be traced to an inversion of remarkably similar nature in hermetic writings of the alchemists. Paul Naudon[14] describes this Christian manifestation of mystic reversal in values:

> Christ says to St. John, "I am the Alpha and
> the Omega," which in Greek numbering...would
> be...108.
> The Greek word for dove...has the numerical
> value of 801. This number [is] attributed to the
> Holy Ghost, ...the Hermetic doctrine of unity.

---

[14] Reinhard Federmann, *The Royal Art of Alchemy* (Philadelphia: Chilton Book Co., 1969).

In the following scene, III, iv, at the seduction of Beatrice, De Flores draws her to him:

> Come, rise and shroud your blushes in .my
> bosom...'las! how the turtle [dove] pants!

The Holy Ghost (801): Beatrice (701). And Christ (108): De Flores (107); feminine in the descendant, masculine in the ascendant: the declension of the divine to the grossly human.

And as to the hermetic unity of their fusing we have just heard De Flores instruct his accomplice in murder:

> Y' are the deed's creature....
> Peace and innocency has turn'd you out,
> And made you one with me.

The volatile tongue of fire, of faith, is here degraded to the faithless heat of lust. And this we are to find is to be the inversionary path of descent followed by Rowley and Middleton in their symbolic employment of the other two occult sciences of the Chaldeans to the blood-dipped lovers, a path down to astrological and alchemic debasement.

In contemplating the astrological symbolism which forms a schema by which the action of the final act is ordered, we now return to Lollio's recital of the hours. This conceit is derived, as noted, from the then very popular sequence of the hours in *The Kalendar of Shepherds*. In the popular mind the seven-hour passage through the planetary sequence marked the shepherds' night-long vigil at the birth of Christ while the Magi, wise men of the East possessed of arcane Chaldean knowledge, journeyed to the manger. *The Changeling*'s violent appropriation of this sequence, marking the holy vigil to the service of the final act's fiery death of virginity and actual death by fire of the virginal Diaphanta, effects a shocking inversion of the sacred to the profane.

As voiced by Lollio, *The Kalendar's* sequence proceeds from eye to belly, the sequence of lust pursued by Beatrice who, with the play's opening line, begins in the temple and thereafter sinks to belly sports with the lubricious De Flores whose "thoughts are at a banquet," there to enjoy "all sweets that darkness ever tasted" (III, iv) as he anticipates the surfeit of sensual delights he is to enjoy with her.

> LOLLIO: ...for every part has his hour:
> we wake at six and look about, that's eye-hour;
> at seven we should pray, that's knee-hour;
> at eight walk, that's leg-hour;
> at nine gather flowers and pluck a rose,
>     that's nose-hour;
> at ten we drink, that's mouth-hour;
> at eleven lay about us for victuals,
>     that's hand-hour;
> at twelve go to dinner, that's belly-hour.

Acts IV and V follow this symbolic sequence. Act IV covers the "seven hours to bed time," midnight, when Alsemero is to couple with his supposed virgin bride, (Beatrice-) Joanna. Between Acts IV and V Diaphanta, yet another "changeling," one substituted for another (she in a bed-trick), willingly couples in the dark at the cost of her virginity. Act V presents a ritualistically strict ordering of the hours: the clock strikes one, then two, then three; thereafter two actions of searing significance complete the degradation of Beatrice. The total action, then, of the final act and the lead-in subplot action at the close of IV coincides astrologically under planetary governance with *The Kalendar* thusly:

> the eleventh hour: leg-hour,
> midnight: nose-hour,
> one o'clock: mouth-hour,
> two o'clock: hand-hour,
> three o'clock: belly-hour, under Mercury,
> the fourth hour: eye-hour, under Luna,
> and the fifth hour: knee-hour, under Saturn.

Textual evidence supports this sequence of bodily functions governing Beatrice's ultimate abasement in cringing supplication, on her knees.

The eleventh hour, leg-hour, involves in the closing scene of IV a heavy load of allusion relating to an action of "treading": Isabella, the subplot's feminine target equivalent to Beatrice in the main action, limns the figure of descent that is to engulf Beatrice. Echoing Beatrice's cry of despair as she is ensnared in the seductive coils of De Flores— "I am in a labyrinth" (III, iv) —Isabella, dressed as a madwoman, employs the infernal Dantean figure:

> And let us tread the lower labyrinth;
> I'll bring thee to the clue.

Midnight, nose-hour, is anticipated by Lollio's indelicate remark that, as organizer of the madhouse capers, he will see to it that at the third-night's revels (in yet another inversion of the action of Christ: "And on the third night he descended to the living,") the pretended madman, Franciscus, shall "pluck a rose," that is to say, have his ease, with Isabella: "Well I'll give you over then, and she shall cast your water."

One o'clock, mouth-hour, finds Beatrice availing herself of gustatory imagery in venting her pique at her waiting woman's overlong lying with her spouse in the exercise of the bed-trick:

> One struck, and yet she lies by 't!...
> This strumpet...
> Devours the pleasure with a greedy appetite...

Two o'clock, hand-hour: the text here makes explicit reference to the body part:

> DE FLORES: ...You're undone;
> The day-star, by this hand! See, Phosphorus...
> BEATRICE: Advise me now to fall upon some reach.
> DE FLORES: This is my reach: I'll set
> Some part afire of Diaphanta's chamber.

As in the inversion of the Christian tongue of fire which brought Faith to the world, as woman descended with her faithlessness, we here have its reversal: woman falls, man strives to rise, though the fire he holds forth is here not the amatory but its opposite, the destructive, the devouring. It is a figure that looks to the ensuing symbol, the center of voracious appetite.

Three o'clock: belly-hour, under Mercury. Diaphanta finally emerges from the darkened bridal chamber. Her satiety gives cause for her to sigh "I never made / So sweet a bargain." With that she exits to her death. We are reminded that this likening of the liaison to a sweet comestible is the selfsame figure De Flores employed in his savoring the anticipated pleasures of Beatrice, "all sweets that darkness ever tasted." Then, as De Flores returns from his deadly mission, we again encounter the image of a consuming fire.

> DE FLORES: Now the flames are greedy of her;
> burnt, burnt, burnt to death.

Torch in hand, he had rushed to Diaphanta's chamber to dispatch her lest she reveal that she, not Beatrice, had lain with Alsemero on the wedding night. He was akin to the figure of Mercury; for, as the master of the occult, Claudius Ptolemy, observed: Mercury "represents a man...able by his genius to produce wonders." One might imagine Beatrice had this astral image in mind as she exclaimed admiringly at De Flores' mercurial dispatch:

> How rare is that man's speed!
> ...Here's a man worth loving!
> ...A wondrous necessary man...

With the coming of the fourth hour, we enter the final scene, V. iii. Now the astrological schema underlying the action moves toward the close. At this point Rowley takes over from Middleton. There is no shift in metaphor. Theirs is a very intimate collaboration.

The fourth-hour, eye-hour, under Luna, marks the change in Beatrice, as she is seen by the "intellectual eyesight," the "eyes of judgment" (II, i). She, woman, the silver eye of night, suffers a failure of nerve, an eclipse of her blood. She betrays her passion. She, as Luna, who had led lovers to lunacy, as the subplot revealed (III, iii):

> LOLLIO: And Luna made you mad...
> FRANCISCUS: Luna is now big-bellied...

she, as Luna, who had "waxed" (IV, iii) while passion raged:

> ISABELLA: Oh heaven! Is this the waxing moon?

now goes dark:

> ALSEMERO: What an opacous body had that moon
> That last chang'd on us.

And the cause of her darkening—her womanly hypocrisy in a prideful claim to murder as cover for her whoredom:

> BEATRICE: To your bed's scandal
> stand up innocence, ...the guilt of
>     one other black deed
> Will stand for proof of: your love has made me
> A cruel murd'ress.

Alsemero, a narrow spirit, cannot gauge the depth of her descent. He the outraged husband only sees her betrayal and insult to his manhood: "Here's beauty chang'd/To ugly whoredom." An innocent who would enshrine his love, he cannot heed the truth the secret arts of nature reveal. He could not credit the gnomic wisdom bespoken by Claudius Ptolemy: "Luna makes one susceptible of change." Luna, who rules the shifting tides; woman, mistress of aqueous mutability. He did not heed in his life the malevolent astrological prognostic expressed by his friend, Jasperino: " 'Tis the critical day, it seems, and the sign of Aquarius," nor the ominous warning of the servant on seeing approach the ship bearing Beatrice: "... this smoke will bring forth fire." Rather he "sees," from his confined vantage, only the visage of a bride blasted: "Oh, thou art all deformed! ...Here's beauty chang'd/To ugly whoredom."

With the fifth, and final, hour, knee-hour, under Saturn, we see the debasement of Beatrice, her "change" in essence, a change that lowers her to the blacker black of utter ignorance. Cornelius Agrippa in *Anima Astrologiae* describes her fallen state: "The moon...if she be void of light and with Saturn, ...is ['a fool'] indeed."

An arcane knowledge of the stance of Saturn, the dark planet, would then have made evident to the traffickers in the black arts (and there were many in the theater of Rowley and Middleton) the gesture of Saturn is a bowing of the knee. Beatrice bows. She humbles herself, abases herself before society. Indeed, she is "a fool."

BEATRICE: Forgive me, Alsemero, all forgive!

She, the moon, "big-bellied" and "waxing" in the silver flush of passion, sinks to "fathoms bottomless" under the governance of Saturn, the leaden planet.

For Beatrice is "the Changeling." We have had hints of it in the text's allusions to the mystic inversions on the numerological and astrological schemata. In the closing action Rowley engages the powers of darkness: he introduces a fury of figures drawn from the noble art of alchemy, figures which, to initiates into the mysteries of the art, create splendid horror at the utterness of her degradation. For Rowley presents us with the image of a woman who is suffered to undergo inversion to the basest element. She, silver, becomes as lead. The seven-phased process of alchemic refinement is reversed. We end, not as Alsemero hoped at the opening, with perfection: "So there's beginning and perfection." We end, rather, with the state of absolute corruption—with the state of nigredo.

Basilius Valentinus has written the alchemic formula for the conversion of base into precious metal: "Unite the fugitive female with the fixed male." Rowley unites them in a dark retort; they are driven within the closet by Alsemero, there to

> ...rehearse again
> Your scenes of lust, that you may be perfect
> When you come to act it to the black audience,

there "to sink to fathoms bottomless." (Enter De Flores, bringing in Beatrice wounded.) Then, in a speech of gelid horror she abases herself before her father.

> Oh come not near me, sir, I shall defile you!
> I am that of your blood was taken from you
> For your better health; look no more upon 't,
> But cast it to the ground regardlessly,
> Let the common sewer take it from distinction:
> Beneath the stars, upon yon meteor
> Ever hung my fate, 'mongst things corruptible.

She dies, a plea for forgiveness on her lips, a plea that is not granted. This "bride within a seven night," who would wait breathless with murder and lost maidenhood the "seven hours to bed time," receives no surcease in her torment. The last voice she hears as she is about to die is that of "the basilisk":

> [*Stabbing himself*] Make haste, Joanna, be that token to thee
> (Thou canst not forget—so lately put in mind)
> I would not go to leave thee far behind. [*Dies.*]

The use of the action verb "go" in this context startles one. It has a familiar resonance. Might it not bring a "strange pedantry" to bear as Symons so well states it was Rowley's wont to do? We have in the inversion of the alchemic process to the leaden state of corruption, of blackness, in the contrition of Beatrice but the penultimate phase. The lead must sink, to "hell," or, in the Dantean metaphor Rowley employed in his "silly" underplot (IV, iii), the lovers are to "tread the lower labyrinth." Though, again in a reversal of conventional order in this black rite, it is man, the serpent, the agent of change, who leads woman (Beatrice) into the labyrinthine depths.

In this account of Rowley's, and Middleton's, brilliant achievement in structuring a series of symbolic schemata of staggering complexity, there has been little respect paid the language, the vigor of the language.

Perhaps it is that my ear is not tuned to hear the "roughness" in Rowley's lines some critics have chided; rather, in the most tragic of moments I sense a Rowleyan tonic abruptness that imparts a strange upward turn to the sinking line of feeling. Instance: the strange elation one experiences at De Flores' death, in capping a rhymed couplet:

> (Thou canst not forget—so lately put in mind)
> I would not go to leave thee far behind.

And again, over the bodies, and amid the race of punning conceits describing how all have "changed" (though well we know the only change of moment is in the heroine, Beatrice-

Joanna, who is dashed from Euripidean heights), we hear intoned by the brother of the slain Piracquo another line which recalls that "strange pedantry" of Rowley.

> TOMAZO: Those black fugitives...are fled from hence

"Fled," again, as with "go," an allusion to action through space. Perhaps the fineness of the pattern may prove too much to credit, yet I cannot help seeing in this final action of the two lovers, descending the coils leading to the bottomless abyss, allusion to the next hour in the cycle of the *Kalendar*:

> LOLLIO: ...at eight walk, that's leg hour...

When Rowley framed this action some three hundred and fifty years ago he set the "twins of mischief" in endless motion. They tread the lower labyrinth still, united in blackness. While to many it may seem an unacceptable extravagance to project beyond the time frame of a dramatic action, I cannot help wondering if the fixed male who united with the volatile female has led her to the clue, for I cannot help believing Rowley would not have left them unhappily in the stern "hell" of Vermandero. Rather, theirs would appear more justly to be the "hell" of the game of barley-brake, wherein the last couple are "left in hell" (together). The comic spirit of Rowley, and Middleton (for that they collaborated at all stages I have no doubt at all, so perfect is their interplay, so harmoniously just the subtle discords of their lines), would not deny these lovers who loved too well, and wisely, in the deepest sense, their body pleasures—even beyond the grave.

For does not the final line from the sober lips of Alsemero counsel so?

> Man and his sorrow at the grave must part.

De Flores would have her "blood to understand" him (III, iv). Might not she, "the changeling," come to understand, blood mingling, in the dark.

# *"Riders to the Sea"*
# *Reappraised*
## (with Martin Bryan)

Then to the depths!—I could as well say height:
Follow it down, it leads you to the Mothers.
Goethe, *Faust I*

trs. MacNeice and Wayne

John Millington Synge's *Riders to the Sea* is conventionally regarded as a model of naturalistic drama. We feel this valuation requires reappraisal, one which sees beyond the ostensibly naturalistic surface and which takes into account Synge's research readings and background writings, as well as expert testimony as to Synge's nature.

In pursuing this attempt at a reappraisal of *Riders to the Sea* we shall first consider what, on the evidence, Synge is not, then consider what Synge is. Next we shall consider the sources Synge consulted in writing *Riders*. Finally, upon the basis of this groundwork, we shall offer what, in our estimation, *Riders to the Sea* is.

*What Synge Is Not*

John Gassner in *Masters of the Drama* obviously felt some reservation, we gather, about including Synge among the masters, having remarked: "Synge lacked only the comprehensiveness of a great dramatist of ideas, and this is his greatest limitation."[1] Continuing along this line, Una Ellis-Fermor, in *The Irish Dramatic Movement*, noted that in Synge "there is no relating of the world of men with... [the] metaphysical universe."[2] And hitting the same note, we have Alan Price in *Synge and Anglo-Irish Drama* remarking upon Synge's lack of metaphysical implications:

> Although it is probably true that the work of the greatest artists have metaphysical and religious implications, the lack of such is not to be thought of necessarily as a flaw in Synge as an artist; it suggests that he is not among the greatest, that there may be limitations in his outlook as a man, but it does nothing more.[3]

We feel it does quite enough. It assumes the critic has exhausted the possible meanings and found them wanting. Continuing in this negative vein, Ronald Peacock, in *The Poet in the Theatre*, apparently thinks Synge rates as a poet but not as a philosopher, for, in his view, "Synge's effect quite transcends the miniature scale on which he is working.... *Riders to the Sea* has nothing whatever of the complexity of the tragic processes in human life that we find handled and mastered by the greatest writers."[4] In sum, Synge might be granted an outer room in the hall of the great, a drafty corner perhaps. How

[1] John Gassner, *Masters of the Drama* (New York: Dover Publications, 1945).

[2] Una Ellis-Fermor, *The Irish Dramatic Movement* (London: Methuen & Co., 1939).

[3] Alan Price, *Synge and Anglo-Irish Drama* (London: Methuen, 1961).

[4] Ronald Peacock, *The Poet in the Theatre* (London: Routledge, 1946).

easily Synge is dismissed! Hear Raymond Williams in his *Drama from Ibsen to Eliot:* "In *Riders to the Sea* the people are simply victims.... [We see] man in the simple exercise of his routine existence. The tragedy is natural, in the most common sense of that term...simply an issue of observation and record."[5] Such is the facile dismissal. Yet who is to say this is simply an issue of observation and record? We wish to be excluded from this superior chorus; we refuse to be party to this devaluing of Synge.

Nevertheless, strongly though we may disagree with Williams and the others, it is necessary, in all fairness, to include a negative verdict on *Riders* which Synge himself rendered. In 1909, near the close of his short life (and perhaps illness may explain the dejected tone), Synge wrote:

> *Riders to the Sea* is a mere commonplace story of unrelieved trouble and grief—"trouble on trouble, pain on pain"— combined with what, for want of a better name, we call bad luck. But I can't see anything very striking or interesting in the expression of it, or certainly, anything that is worthy to be called dramatic. It is mere conversation, not drama. But the *Manchester Guardian* calls it "a tragic masterpiece of our language in our time"! Perhaps, after all, that is not saying much. I hardly read enough to be able to judge; but I apprehend there is not much great tragedy written in these islands ["England" crossed out] nowadays.

Synge, in making this confession of sorts, went against the grain of his declared conviction that, according to Goethe, one should "tell no one what one means in one's writings." It also was at odds with Synge's well-stated view that "all theorizing is bad for the artist, because it makes him live in the intelligence instead of the half-subconscious faculties by which all creation

---

⁵ Raymond Williams, *Drama from Ibsen to Eliot* (London: Chatto & Windus, 1952).

is performed." Further, artists are often poor witnesses of the depths contained in their work; of this Synge himself was aware, for he placed the creative unconscious above critical consciousness. As G. Wilson Knight noted:

> "Intentions" belong to the plane of the intellect and memory: the swifter consciousness that awakens in poetic composition touches subtleties and heights and depths unknowable by the intellect and intractable to memory.[6]

In closing this brief consideration of what, in our view, Synge is not, we are hopeful that the foregoing has given grounds for challenging the generally held prejudice that Synge was but a mere reporter. We are further hopeful that the consideration of what we feel Synge to be will offer some basis for the contention that *Riders to the Sea* is much more than a documentary record; is, in fact, a manifestation of an inner vision, a brilliant upthrust from the substrata of Synge's creative unconscious, an unconscious which he, with all poets, knows with the deepest sort of "knowing."

*What Synge Is*

To begin with, J.M. Synge's inner fire was anything but Christian. In Denis Johnston's very brief biography, Synge is described as an "anticlerical descendant of Anglican bishops."[7] Synge's autobiographical novel (titled *My Youth* in its published version), written in the mid-1890s, bears this out, having this revealing passage: "By the time I was sixteen or seventeen I had renounced Christianity. For a while I denied everything.

---

[6] G. Wilson Knight, *The Wheel of Fire* (London: Oxford University Press, 1930).

[7] Denis Johnston, *John Millington Synge* (New York: Columbia University Press, 1965).

Then I...made myself a sort of incredulous belief that illuminated nature." In this Yeats, who was himself fully sympathetic
with the mystic dimensions of experience, found in Synge a
spirit akin to his own, having noted regarding Synge that he
"was a drifting man full of hidden passion [who] loved wild
islands because there...he saw what lay hidden in himself."[8]

We recall that it was Yeats who in Paris told Synge, then
suffering the frustrations of a neglected artist, to leave the
effete circle in Paris and venture to the furthermost islands in
the West, the Aran Islands. There Synge was to find, in the
summers through 1902, material to vent the violent passions
Yeats saw burning in his dark friend. These sojourns were to
find their outcome in *Riders*. We might further recall that
through the long winters Synge returned to Paris, to its brilliant circle of expatriate Irish writers—to such talents as Yeats
and Stephen MacKenna, most of all to MacKenna, self-taught
genius, translator of Plotinus' *Enneads*. With this closest of his
friends, Synge spent the many long nights talking of literature
and the supernatural, as MacKenna's memoirs fondly relate.
And that their converse touched on Synge's reflections on the
powers in nature may be gleaned from the fact that his letters to
MacKenna were later seriously mutilated in what MacKenna's
biographer, Eric Robertson Dodds, terms the excision of
"blasphemous" material. That nature mysticism was a continuing interst of Synge's we have his own testimony in his notebook of 1907, he having then observed that "our modern
feeling for the...mystery of nature...has gradually risen up as
religion in the dogmatic sense has gradually died." MacKenna
had a similar outlook, writing that "if the consecrated religions
are doomed to pass away...there will still be mystics and mysticism...strange forms of lawless, emotional religion."[9] What this

---

[8] W. B. Yeats, *Synge and the Ireland of His Time* (Churchtown, Dun-
drum: The Cuala Press, 1911).

[9] *Journal and Letters of Stephen MacKenna*, ed. Eric Robertson Dodds
(London: Constable & Co., 1936).

"lawless, emotional religion" might have entailed we can only surmise, but Synge hinted at its dark content in his notebook: "The sexual element...exists in all really fervent ecstasies of faith...[that reign] in pagan forests of the south." And Synge, in his autobiography, further elaborated on the theme, writing of the "powerful hypnotic suggestions of earth upon prepared personalities." In these expressions Synge reflected his turning away from the religion of churches to face the elemental nature forces. In this movement he was not unique: he was party to the swing of sentiment current at the turn of the century, a swing away from the civilized and toward the primal. Lines from an unpublished play Synge wrote in 1901 are part of this chthonic surge: "In the Christian synthesis each separate faculty has been dying of atrophy.... The only truth a wave knows is that it is going to break.... The only truth we know is that we are a flood of magnificent life, the fruit of some frenzy of the earth." Such lines as these, Greene/Stephens note in their biography, were "reflection of the utterance Synge had shocked his mother with."[10] Such fervor had not shocked Yeats; this we can gather from his commenting upon his friend as "conceiving the world as if it were an overflowing caldron," as one "ready to sacrifice every convention, perhaps all that men have agreed to reverence, for a startling theme." Such was the intensity of Synge's spirit that Yeats was moved to remark upon his "hunger for harsh facts, for surprising things, for all that denies our hope.... Benign images ever present to his soul must have beside them malignant reality, and the greater the brightness the greater the darkness must be." The light, the dark; the positive, the negative; the male, the female—the list of polarized antagonists is framable in many couplings. And of this host engendered from such opposition contained in the tormented soul of Synge, a heat intensified by the repressions upon normal outlet inflicted

---

[10] David H. Greene and Edward M. Stephens, *J. M. Synge* (New York: Macmillan, 1959).

by the repressions of Irish social mores, Yeats took note in writing that Synge's "was the rushing up of the buried fire, an explosion of all that had been denied or refused."

And what was true of Synge is true of his Ireland. Such damming of natural passions finds release in violence. Synge sensed this subterranean swell: "There is hardly an hour I am with them [the Aran Islanders] that I do not feel the shock of some inconceivable idea found in the oldest poetry and legend."

*Synge's Sources for* Riders of the Sea:

The works Synge took with him to Aran indicate that he was anything but innocent, anything but a superficial witness of surfaces. Clearly he was in the mainstream of Parisian thought, fully *au courant* with the arts and letters of his time, with symbolism. In the Greene/Stephens biography we find he took with him Paulam's *Nouveau Mysticisme*, the *Proceedings of Psychical Research*, Maeterlinck (of whose "transcendental" approach he had commented in a Parisian review), A.E.'s *Earth Breath*, as well as Swedenborg. Most significantly, he took with him Pierre Loti's *An Island Fisherman*, a novel of French romanticism. In it Synge read of the sea as an attracting and devouring force. Here he encountered "the boundless regions of that attracting, fascinating, devouring thing...the polar seas," "great nurse and...great destroyer." In it he found the sea as generative and dissolving force, its "rage...causeless, aimless, as mysterious as life, as mysterious as death."

These were the works Synge took with him to *Creaga Dubha*, Black Crag. With them as reading companions he conceived of the dark action of *Riders to the Sea*. For *Riders* does not celebrate the burst of light, the emergence from the darkness; rather it celebrates the engulfment in darkness. His dialogue is permeated with shadow. Maurya intones: "I'll have no call to be going down and getting Holy water in the dark nights after Samhain. It isn't that I haven't said prayers in the dark night till you wouldn't know what I'ld be saying." The reference to Samhain is crucial; it relates the action to a major source for the drama: the archaic rites of the Irish calendar.

Samhain was a pagan feast transferred to the Christian calendar, the feast of the dead, Halloween, the transitional time marking the shift from the period of growth to that of decay and death. Into the central darkness of Samhain Maurya descended, and with her, her sons, her husband, and his father before him. So descended the sacrificial victims in the awful rite of pagan Samhain, for then it was that the Druids assembled to sacrifice and burn their human offering. Of this pagan shadow the Aran Islands have contemporary trace: on Inishere are the remains of a great pagan burial ground. Further, the very church at Kilmurvey was originally a pagan fortress, and the church itself gives witness to an earlier pagan faith: over its fount of holy water is a Norman *mememto mori*. Of such pagan reminders of mortality we have comment in Loti's *An Island Fisherman*: below an inscription on a funeral tablet commemorating the loss of a ship's crew were "two cross-bones under a black skull" suggestive of "the barbarism of a bygone age." If it be doubted that such pagan elements from his environment, real and literary, did in fact impinge on Synge's consciousness during his stay on the islands, such doubt fades when it is recalled that he wrote of "the simple prayer for the dead" he heard "spoken by voices that were still hoarse with cries of pagan desperation." Pagan memory still exists on Aran. This, Synge knew. And Samhain would naturally come to the mother's mind; thought of it was natural to her, for at Samhain the Celtic *Matres*, the earthgoddesses and spirits of the corn, as E.O. James notes in *Seasonal Feasts and Festivals*, "together with the spirits of the dead, were feasted and placated and their aid...sought to bring life and light out of the prevailing darkness...anticipated at Samhain."[11] Pursuing

---

[11] E. O. James, *Seasonal Feasts and Festivals* (London: Thames and Hudson, 1961).

this maternal aspect of the Samhain sacrifice, J.A. MacCulloch in *The Religion of the Ancient Celts,* has related how, in the Celtic past, "Christmas eve was called *Modranicht,* 'Mother's Night,' and as many of the rites of Samhain were transferred to Yule, the former date of *Modranicht* may have been Samhain."[12] The eve of life to the Christian world, the eve of death to the archaic faith: such is the fusion effected possibly on the "earth" MacKenna felt "heaving with divinity." Further, Whitley Stokes in *Revue Celtique* (1882)[13] pursued the matter of the pagan Irish worship of the mothers even more closely to the mystery at the center of *Riders to the Sea.* Etymologically he related the great mother, Morrigan, with Formarian, the Celtic nightmare queen. This relating of the great mother to the nightmare hag is of crucial importance to an understanding of the mother in Synge's play; without this connection her ritualistic actions over the body of her last son would lack significance. The action to which we refer: Maurya's placing her hands upon the feet of the dead Bartley and her turning the cup mouth downwards upon the table.

## *What* Riders to the Sea *Is*

*Riders to the Sea* is a mystery. Its meaning lies beneath its dramatic surface. It deals with motives which lie hidden deep in man's unconscious, motives the existence of which are seldom grasped but which, despite their lack of social sanction, emerge as dream fantasy upthrusts from the substrata of man's collective existence. Carl Jung framed the theory of the archetypes of the collective unconscious, and his structure contains the essential nature of *Riders to the Sea:* it is an archetypal mystery, a mystery of the duality infusing all, of the mystic union of opposites, the *coincidentia oppositorum* of the alchemists and

[12] J.A. MacCulloch, *The Religion of the Ancient Celts* (Edinburgh: T. & T. Clark, 1911).

[13] Whitley Stokes, "Notes sur des textes Irlandais," *Revue Celtique* (1882).

mystics. It marks a dramatic realization of the resolution of the conflict between the existent and the nonexistent, between object and void. At this metaphysical level, *Riders to the Sea* is far beyond the ultimate Christian concept of an unalterably divided duality. This view is shared by Denis Johnston, who has written that the play "is neither pious nor basically Christian.... No moral choice at all is offered to the characters; the sea—not the Gods—is the source of the law in this play, and there is no escape from it." The sea *is* the master (or mistress) of the action. Yet there is a counter action: the riding of the men (and women) down to the sea. The deaths of Maurya's sons, husband, and his father before him, are enactments of the rite of confrontation and dissolution in the eternal drama of existence played upon the ground of the void. Maurya, the mother in the play, who gives her family to the sea, is more than mother, more than succorer, more than vessel which brings man into existence; she is also the receptacle in which he finds his terminal dissolution. Woman, the play reveals at its deepest level, is more than a creative force: she is also destructive. An awareness of this metaphysic is evidenced in Alan Price's intimation that the atavistic hunger of the void for all creation is embodied in Maurya. It led him to write that Maurya "feels that the sea, the hunger for destruction at the heart of the universe, is too powerful for the antidotes of religion." Although Price does not note it, the heart of the matter is here touched upon. Maurya more than feeling the hunger of the sea, *is* the sea. Seen in this light, it is her hunger for the destruction of the men that is at the heart of their self-sacrifice, a hunger satiated from the evidence of the symbolic gestures she makes over her last son.

Maurya, the mother, had hinted at the darkness informing her action, having cried out: "It isn't that I haven't said prayers in the dark night till you wouldn't know what I'ld be saying." This cry of despair, with its hint of blasphemy or pagan celebration, is an echo, we find, of *An Island Fisherman*, these the words that Synge might well have read: "Poor old woman ...to show at last...[that] which had all her life lain dormant; such a knowledge of dark words, which had been concealed...what a mocking mystery!" Maurice Bourgeois, it bears emphasizing, has noted that Synge took *An Island Fisherman* to the Aran Island with him as a source for *Riders* because of its "psychological merits and...all-pervading notion of impending terror."[14] And of the women's blending of Christian resignation with pagan fury we have Synge's own words in *The Aran Islands*. Writing of the keening of the women he noted that in its forlorn rage it "seemed to contain the whole passionate rage that lurks somewhere in every native of the islands...the mood of beings who feel their isolation in the face of a universe that wars on them with winds and seas...the terror of the world." This "terror of the world," might it not be the very terror of which Loti wrote when he noted the grandmother's "thought wandered away into that attracting, fascinating, devouring thing...the polar seas...the ever-present sea, the great nurse and the great destroyer of the vigorous generations"? And might not the cold terror of the Arctic seas, "the great nurse and destroyer," have penetrated the racial unconscious of the Eddic *scöps* who sang with tightened throats of the nightmare hag, the *mara* (pronounced maw-rah) which, as described in the Icelandic *Heimkringla* saga, "went to [the King's] head and legs in turn, breaking his legs and smothering him, so that he died"? Might not the terror have rooted in Synge's being when he was led to describe Maurya's strangely formal gesture over Bartley:

> *Maurya puts the empty cup mouth downwards on the table and lays her hands together on Bartley's feet.*

And might there have been more than a terror in Synge as he

<hr>

[14] Maurice Bourgeois, *John Millington Synge and the Irish Theatre* (London: Constable, 1913).

saw this mother exercise her dark rite over her son? For Synge, in his notebook, exulted that in the eyes of the women of Aran he had found "the whole symphony of sky and seas."

Morrigan, the great mother; Mara, the nightmare figure—fused in the mother, Maurya; she, the fused duality that is woman.

But *Riders to the Sea* extends beyond this psychic syncretism. It fuses the horror of this symbolic act of destruction with Maurya's symbolic words of resignation: "No man can be living forever and we must be satisfied." From the mystical perspective these words have nothing to do with Christian resignation: it may express, rather, quite literally, a resigning (f. L.: *resignare*), unsealing of all existents of man's imagining, of man's creation—quite literally, a cancelling of all accounts.

Though Maurya, we suggest may in her ritualistic gestures be a paradigmatic figure of the fused duality that is woman, the encompassing "circlic" whole, the mother image celebrated in the myths of Parvati-Kali, Demeter-Hecate, the play, in its total action is a paradigm of the fused duality that cancels out, the fused duality that "is" the void.

In *Riders to the Sea* Synge plunged down the dark and convolute passage. In it he celebrated a psychic declension in a rite enacting the centripetal pull of the void. A psychic tragedy of declension and separation—this we find *Riders to the Sea*; and more! a psychic comedy of ascension and consummation. As Goethe stated:

Then to the depths!—I could as well say height: Follow it down, it leads you to the Mothers.

Morrigan-Mara-Maurya: mother of all, mystery of the archetypal (w)hole.

# The Möbius Path and Dürrenmatt's "The Physicists"

Friedrich Dürrenmatt's *The Physicists* (1964) is the kind of play critics have difficulty warming to on short acquaintance. Finding it abstract, a play of ideas, they gave it short shrift at its London opening; reviews faulted its obscurity. Time has not seen the harsh judgment of opening night amended. In the past decade the play has received scant attention; no strenuous attempt has been made to penetrate beyond its ostensibly humanistic sympathies. George Wellwarth, fitting it into his major thesis took it to be a humanist tract: "Dürrenmatt's protest...is not against the cosmos: it is against the world as it is and against the people who rule it."[1] Murray B. Peppard, in his book on Dürrenmatt, also has seen it simplistically, having written of how it teaches a "lesson" demonstrating "...the impossibility of reforming the world and reversing the course

---

[1] George Wellwarth, *The Theatre of Protest and Paradox* (New York: New York University Press, 1964).

106

of history."[2] Yet Peppard has sensed a more extensive range of thought in Dürrenmatt, finding him to be "...an author engaged in a struggle with nihilism." Peppard was onto something here, yet when he came to consider *The Physicists* this insight was lost and we have from him a reproof of Dürrenmatt, the technician (and, by implication, of Dürrenmatt the thinker), for he curtly censured his handling of the opening stage directions: "Totally irrelevant details...are supplied for no apparent reason except delight in enumeration.... It seems as if Dürrenmatt's baroque urges...had...found an outlet in stage directions."

It is alarming to find, in a substantial critical study, such a superficial (or so it shall be the burden of this chapter to prove) derogation of a proven master. It is truly dismaying when one gives the text of the play a close reading. Upon such examination, I suggest, the construction of *The Physicists* will be found exemplary. The play, when it is viewed as more than a mad dance of frustrate science, comes into focus as a network of concepts of forbidding complexity. It would not do to scant the difficulties the play poses: it is a mystery drama, and its secrets are well concealed, so much so that one can only begin to frame philosophic schemata to give shape to the intricacies of the action by careful reference to the details contained in the published version of the play.[3] For, I propose, *the* key to an understanding of the intricate concepts underlying the action lies in the seeming irrelevancies of the very scene directions scored so sharply by Peppard.

In the first act, upon the entrance of the play's antagonist, Fräulein Doktor Mathilde von Zahnd, a fact of more than passing interest is noted: "—*her correspondence with C.G. Jung has just been published*." This datum, in the context of an action which pits her against the protagonist, an atomic scien-

---

[2] Murray B. Peppard, *Friedrich Dürrenmatt* (New York: Twayne Publishers, 1969).

[3] *The Physicists*, tr. James Kirkup (New York: Grove Press, 1964).

tist significantly bearing the name of Möbius, might, one
would expect, have set critical minds turning. Möbius: Jung
—how might they relate? What has the mathematician, discov-
erer of the single surface figure, the Möbius band, posthum-
ously published in 1868, to do with Jungian philosophy?

While there is some justification for the commonly expressed
view that a play should not require a resort to the library for its
meaning to emerge, and some may well feel that reference to
the collected works of a prolific scholar (Jung) is to put a rather
heavy damper on enjoyment of the play as theater, such an
attitude is hardly defensible. Plays are also for the study.
Surely, an awareness of pattern is a major source of aesthetic
and intellectual delight. When Jung's works on the psyche, the
inner cosmos of mental energies, are brought into play on the
field of physical force Dürrenmatt has fashioned in *The Physicists*, such a pattern as Peppard described in the corpus of the
author, a "nihilist" pattern, will be discovered.

Dürrenmatt, in his "Problems of the Theatre", conceived of
just such a psychic drama of "inner space."[4] Some half dozen
years later he realized this concept on the stage. *The Physicists*
is a drama which finds its intellectual impetus in Jung's psychic
research. No claim is here made that the following analysis
exhausts the Jungian sources. Therefore, that the reader, in his
search for possible connections between Möbius and Jung,
may have a start on such relevancies as I have discerned, the
volumes from Jung's collected works which bear on *The Physicists* are: *Aion* (1959), *Psychology and Alchemy* (1953),
*Alchemical Studies* (1967, given in lecture at Eranos Conference in 1942), *Symbols of Transformation* (1956),[5] and, as well,

---

[4] *Four Plays*, tr. Gerhard Nellhaus (New York: Grove Press, 1965).

[5] C.G. Jung, *Aion* (1959), *Psychology and Alchemy* (1953), *Alchemical
Studies* (1967), and *Symbols of Transformation* (1956), tr. R.F.C. Hull
(Princeton: Princeton University Press).

"Synchronicity, an Acausal Connecting Principle," in *The Interpretation of Nature and the Psyche.*[6]

The focus of Jung's thought over the years was on the *coincidentia oppositorum*, the fusing of opposites. Two:one —this his preoccupation over a long career of research into mystic trains of thought. Alchemy, the mystery of change, was his obsession. It would seem that the protagonist of *The Physicists*, Möbius, shares Jung's *idée fixe*. He believes he has found the Principle of Universal Discovery. This is closely akin to the final outcome of Jung's long quest for "absolute knowledge," that which, as he noted in "Synchronicity, an Acausal Connecting Principle," is irrepresentable in space-time. Möbius, the scientist in the play, sought unity. Möbius, the scientist in life, sought and found unity in duality—in his simple spatial figure of a band of paper which given a twist and then joined, forms a loop upon which a line can be drawn circling the loop continuously. Result: paradox; an apparently two-sided surface, the paper, has actually but one surface—appearance and reality are confounded. And this we find to be the declared intent of Dürrenmatt: in his appended points at the play's end, point 13 explicitly states, "A play about physicists must be paradoxical."

With Jung, as with the alchemists, Dürrenmatt in his play of inner space sought to confound reason. Where he differs with them is in his ultimate vision: whereas Jung and the alchemists sought an integration of the psyche, Dürrenmatt is engulfed by a black despair of psychic disintegration, of cosmic annihilation.

Contemplate with Dürrenmatt a Möbius band; it is all therein: a paradox of existence, a one-dimensional surface, a Zeno-like linear point, a symbol of infinity. Take a band of paper; twist it once and discover the endless track of infinity. Although it staggers reason, consider existence, the immediacy of this moment, here and now. Does not this point in space cancel the concept of space, as this point in time cancels time?

[6] C.G. Jung, *The Interpretation of Nature and the Psyche*, tr. W. Pauli (New York: Pantheon Books, 1955).

Part/whole: how is one to divide them, and how, in a unity of Being, can there be a many and a one? Is not all one? Yet, is one all? And what of none? At root, this is the mystic paradox. And Dürrenmatt engaged this level of abstraction, and sensed in the image beyond sensing a vacuity which chills the marrow.

> *Möbius*: In the realm of knowledge...we know...a few basic connections between incomprehensible phenomena and that is all. The rest is mystery...we have encountered a void.

"...a few basic connections between incomprehensible phenomena..." This might stand as a definition of the Jungian "acausal connecting principle" of synchronicity. The voiding of the mind when paradox is courted, as in the Möbius band, was experienced by Jung. He, with Dürrenmatt, contemplated cause and irrational effect. Both were drawn to the grotesque paradox, the void behind all: Dürrenmatt in "Problems of the Theatre": "...the form of the unformed, the face of a world without a face," and Jung in "Synchronicity": "A cause is not...thinkable...when space and time lose their meaning." The Möbius strip of non-orientable surface is inconceivable to the rational intellect, as Möbius's life path, as life itself, makes no sense in an indifferent cosmos—or whatever void beyond the void we think we sense exists or does not exist. For, we are again reminded by Jung, in "Synchronicity," who knows his mystic sources well and would have us have ever in mind "the great principle" of Hippocrates, of the "common breathing," the principle of "being and not being."

All these heady paradoxes are intellectual equivalents to the paradox materialized, to the grotesque, which Dürrenmatt ("Problems of the Theatre") declared to be his dramatic aim. And this brings us to a strange conjunction of the reigning principle in Dürrenmatt, the grotesque, and in the Möbius strip which appeared in an article in the *Scientific American*

(January 1950) dealing with topological paradox, and which, in an eerie way, seems more than coincidental, so striking are their points in common. For, in the circumspect pages of this scientific journal we are confronted with a picture of the rampant stone lion which stands beside a fireplace at Princeton, bearing an armorial shield upon which resides—a Möbius strip. The seat of learning where Einstein labored, Princeton, and the paradox of the circular path without beginning or end, the non-orientable surface upon which a fly is seen senselessly crawling. Can it be mere chance that led Dürrenmatt to end his drama of futility in a paean to the very vacuity symbolized in the Princetonian Möbius strip?

> *Möbius*: ...somewhere round a small, yellow,
> nameless star there circles, pointlessly, ever-
> lastingly, the radioactive earth.

The choice would seem attributable to more than mere chance. Einstein is the assumed mask of the second of the mad scientists of the triumvirate peopling Dürrenmatt's nihilistic demonstration. Einstein's theory of relativity destroyed the rational image of space-time, the meaningfulness of a time-locked consciousness, as does Dürrenmatt's closing image of an inverted planetary order deprived of purpose. And, in the fantastic conceit of Dürrenmatt's first act, the Song of Solomon (Möbius's feigned persona) to be sung to the Cosmonauts, we have in astrological form the same figure of logic-confounded, of human purpose excoriated to the point of extinction, as the Princetonian crest whereon a fly crawls endlessly.

> Outcasts we cast out, up into the deep
> Toward a few white stars
> That we never reached anyhow...

Again, the thoughts of Jung come to bear with searing significations. Möbius is, or would be, Solomon. In this regard we note that Jung has observed (*Aion*) that "according to medieval tradition, the religion of the Jews originated in the conjunction of Jupiter and Saturn." Yet the religious resonance is minor; the major significance is beyond the paltry range of theology; the major significance of mysticism is metaphysical. And the overriding symbol for this supreme mystery is not some point in time but the very self-erasing wheel of time itself, the image of the serpent which devours its tail, the uroboros. This we find prominently treated in Jung's studies into alchemy, into the art of psychic para-existent change. It is with a profound shock that, with the Möbius strip in mind, one studies the diagram of the mystic serpent in *Psychology and Alchemy*. Is it not clear that this symbol of Mercurius, the dragon, the tail-eater, "who devours himself...to rise again as the *lapis* [*philosophorum*]" is a Möbius strip? (The twist in the surface of the uroboros from the Codex Marcianus, c. 900-1100, is unmistakable.) Is not the duality of existence unified, the dual appearance of surface existence transcended in the unity? And, if the powers of existence be considered in a Hippocratic dimension, is not the duality of being/non-being transcended in a para-cosmic cancellation? Such a devouring of Being is the alchemic emblem figured in the serpent, and in the lion. Jung would have us know (*Alchemical Studies*): "one of the manifestations of Mercurius in the alchemical process of transformation is the lion, now green and now red." And, again coincidence with Jung is to be found in Dürrenmatt's para-cosmic Song: "From ancient times the lion was associated with Saturn," the lion which devoured the sun, "...the *materia prima* as Saturn [which devoured] his children."

The ultimate paradox: this is Jung's concern, and Dürrenmatt's. The unknown is broached, sense reels. Uroboros, Saturn, Mercurius, emblematic of arcane paradox: "I am known and yet do not exist at all..." (from the "Aurelia occulta," in *Alchemical Studies*).

And as the Cosmonauts, we the human race, venture ever "further" "into" the "outer" reaches of space (how sure we are of our orientation in a field beyond human knowing!), as sensoria penetrate the pleroma and falter in "the void" (how easily the term falls from one's lips) we might, with Dürrenmatt, contemplate the breath of darkness in yet another frame of mystic reference. We might return to the beginning of Western scientific thought and to the shattering concept of another geometer, Pythagoras, who wrote: "The infinite showed itself in the boundless breath of darkness."

With Möbius we might know that we, in the waning light of the West, are

> ...outcasts...
> In our deathsheads no more memories
> Of breathing earth.

All, one, none: lost on the shadow path of Möbius, that is no path.

# The Surprising Unconscious of Edward Albee
## (with Michael Porte)

*I never give a plot away because I'm much more interested in seeing how close the critics come in figuring it out. Anyway, you can't tell what a play's about in a few words. Hopefully it's about more than one thing, there are overtones, and one thought existing on two or three levels.*

*And part of the creative act is surprising yourself. Things work from the unconscious to the conscious.*

Edward Albee in conversation with
John L. Wasserman, June, 1967

Coming across these sentiments of Edward Albee on the primacy of the creative unconscious in the shaping of his work. *A Delicate Balance*, can give one a strange sense of *déjà vu*, for it was during the rehearsals of *Tiny Alice* some two years before that we had report of his having said much to the same effect, "I try to let the unconscious do as much work as possible."

114

Further, his challenge to the critical confraternity resonates familiarly, for in his Author's Note for the printed version of *Tiny Alice* he had similarly observed with regard to the charge that his play was obscure, "I can't understand this as being a complaint about a play.... If a play demands a little bit from the audience...of critics, then I don't think that's a failure on the play's part."

Well, quite a span of time has passed since this challenge was thrown at the critics and they have come up with little beyond their opening night expressions of mystification when Taubman in the *Times* found it "mysterious"; Kerr in the *Herald-Tribune*, "a mystery story of compounded puzzlement"; Nadel in the *World-Telegram*, "a complex mystery"; and Watts in the *Mirror*, "a metaphysical mystery melodrama." One year later Richard Schaap looked with some amusement on this critical vacuum, noting that it had become "a status symbol *not* to understand *Tiny Alice*." Albee himself seems to have joined this select group, having remarked to Sir John Gielgud, "I don't know what it means, yet."

In this dense climate of unknowing it takes some energy to expose oneself with a light of understanding, hopeful of illuminating the obscure corners of Albee's attic, or cellar. (Heraclitus, another trafficker in the mystic having in this context remarked, "Up or down, it's all the same.") Yet this is what we propose to do. For, we advance, *Tiny Alice* is such an exemplification of the workings of the collective unconscious as would cast even Carl Gustav Jung's luminous Miss Miller into the shade.

Jung has had a rather rough time of it on this side; his studies into the archetypal forms of myth have been scored by our hard-nosed behavioral scientists as "unscientific." In support of the beleaguered Jung, we contend, here in a play appropriately named for the goddess of "truth"—*inner* truth — *Aletheia* (Gk., Alice), we have an impressive demonstration of the formative powers of the intuition, and, as well, a total

vindication of Jung's brilliant theory of the collective archetypes as the basis for artistic form. *Tiny Alice*, in brief, is a
working out in dramatic form of Jung.

Archetypes are primal traces; their source is in the earliest
beginnings of the human race. Since the roots of the unconscious go deep into the past, it is understandable that critics,
working from a contemporary vantage point, have failed to see
beyond their narrow and short Judaic-Christian perspectives
into the mystery Albee's unconscious has shaped. Critics, as we
might expect, have identified the play's central character,
Julian, with Christ. Biblical referents, admittedly, have some
degree of relevance; Julian does undergo a symbolic crucifix-
ion. But when one broaches the mystery at the play's core,
Albee somehow appears to be on a different wavelength from
such Christian apologists as Eliot with their repentance and
humility limitations. Somehow, and we won't venture to
hazard how, Albee's unconscious has tuned in on a strange
mid-Eastern theme, one that sounded more than four millennia ago at the birth of the religions of transcendence; he writes
of an escape from the world, from identity and time and
existence. At the end his protagonist, Julian, "accepts" the
deities of the world and its universe, "God" and "Alice." But
the action goes beyond this existent stage to an engulfment of
the world and the universe in absolute silence and utter darkness. To Western minds this may seem a bleak way to end an
evening in the theater. To the initiates of the particular mysteries that Albee through some presently inexplicable parapsychic
process has tapped, it would be otherwise. This mystic sect
views the world as a prison, the universe as an iron vault. To
them, Julian's end in silence and darkness would constitute a
glorious release from the world and from being. Annihilation
of being, this is their ultimate desire. And the puzzling syncretism at the play's close of the Judaeo-Christian "God" and a
mystic triune goddess, "Alice," would to them be clear, as
would also be the descent of a "great presence" in the absolute

annihilation at the curtain. It bears underlining, this utter cancellation of existence is, in the center of the mystery at the core of *Tiny Alice, not* negativistic. At the darkness and silence of the end we are not in the shadow where Beckett dwells. The "great presence" of "Alice" is not that awful presence that closes Beckett's dark drama, *Endgame.* Albee's game goes beyond black checkmate; it goes beyond to the mysteries of Gnosticism, the secret way of knowing. It contains the very mystery of Julian's metaphysical "deliverance" as its central tenet of faith and wisdom.

This brings us to our statement of thesis: we here propose that *Tiny Alice* presents a challenge to faith in the God of Christendom, a challenge which takes the form of a Gnostic ritual whereby the soul is released from existence. Proofs drawn from the characters, actions, and dialogue will follow.

Additionally, we here advance the minor thesis that, beneath the transcendent level of existence, another principle is at work, one drawn from the world of science. With reference to the minor metaphysical puzzle of what Albee has termed his play of "double mystery," we offer that *Tiny Alice* presents a second challenge to Christendom's fundamental beliefs through its realization, in dramatic action, of Sir Isaac Newton's metaphysical theory of etheric inversion, that reversal of value which takes place at what might be described as, quite literally, the point of *reductio ad absurdum.* This, we maintain, will reveal the nature of the otherwise inexplicable change from attraction to repulsion we find in the attitude of Miss Alice toward Julian after her liaison with him in the microcosm at the end of Act II.

We shall thus consider the two climactic rites of *Tiny Alice*: the microcosmic "marriage" of Act II, and the macrocosmic release from existence of Act III. Both, we are convinced, drive at the roots of conventional Christian faith; the earlier and major challenge lodging its assault from the late Roman age when Christendom was about to triumph over Gnostic and other "heretical" faiths which posited a metaphysic of parapsychic transcendence through ecstasy; the later and minor challenge coming from the age of the new science when probing microscopes and telescopes had opened to question the validity of the constricting limits Christendom had set for the intellect and psyche. If there should be doubts about the presence of these challenges in *Tiny Alice*, they should be dispelled by reference to the meaning Albee himself sees in his play. He speaks of it as "a mystery play, a double mystery, and also a morality play, about...easy Gods, all the Gods that we create in our own image." Albee did not elaborate. At this point in the interview it is indicated that he paused and considered, saying finally, "I've said too much." It is a line that might have fallen easily from the lips of Emperor Julian. Indeed, one very similar did just that. But of this more later. We should now wish, before going into a detailed consideration of the play, to capsulize our major and minor theses.

We contend that *Tiny Alice* is, in dramatic form, a demonstration of a psychic transformation in line with Newton's metaphysic (minor thesis), and a Gnostic rite of release from existence (major thesis). Upon examination, we suggest, the play, in its characters, its action, and its dialogue, will disclose the nature of the "double mystery" Albee hinted at: a mystery of metaphysical dimensionality wherein matter is subjected to an inversion of value, and a mystery, unspeakable, wherein existence itself is transcended. The proofs follow.

I. *The Proofs of Character*

    A. Julian, the sacrificial hero-victim in a rite of mystic union with Alice, the cosmic goddess, and a participant in a rite of mystic union-release with the acosmic powers.

Julian bears the name of Emperor Julian, the Apostate. He bears, as well, the Emperor's burden of a questioning intellect, and his gift of mystic vision. Because he "sees" and asks more than his fellow men, he is ridden by doubt. With Julian the Emperor, Julian the lay brother lost sight of the God of the Christians and sought to find a new faith in the fastness of an exile in the interior; both Julians spent identical periods of six years in exile. Both encountered altars aflame. Both, washed by blood, underwent a mystic purificatory rite: the Emperor a rite of initiation into the mysteries of Mithraism; Julian, the lay brother, in an ecstatic dream before his union with the three Alices. And both found release from existence in a secret rite of Gnostic-theurgic annihilation.

In the main figure of *Tiny Alice*, Julian, we thus have one who, with his namesake, sought the secret to the mysteries, and, seeking, found it.

B. Alice, the triune goddess.
  1. Alice

Alice, a name derived from the Greek *Aletheia*, is goddess of truth, of Heideggerian unconcealedness, of hidden wisdom conjoined with faith, the mystic conjunction attained by Julian in his death on her altar. Alice is the intermediary goddess of the Gnostics, reigning in the etheric realm, the seventh sphere of existence. From it the Gnostic initiate attains to the eighth sphere, the acosm, the beyond of absolute silence and darkness.

  2. Miss Alice

Miss Alice is an equivalent to the second, and worldly, aspect of the Gnostic goddess of hidden wisdom who, in a materialization of her divine etheric nature, descended into the prison of the world. Miss Alice, as earthly surrogate to the etheric goddess, Alice, includes within her all humanity and all existents. As the Butler remarks of her: she passes through all that exists, "touching everyone and everything." In essence, she is the universal syzygy. Psychologically considered, she is the fusion of sexes and identities; from the vantage point of astronomic theory, she is the conjunction and opposition of all material existent forces. Of this inner and outer assimilation we have evidence in the act of union at the climax of Act II whereby Julian in the *hieros gamos*, the sacred marriage, simultaneously unites with her microcosmic and macrocosmic forms, with Tiny Alice and with Alice.

Yet, though Miss Alice is absolute earthly being, she is also absolute in her remoteness. In her isolation, in her deep sense of forlorn abandonment in an indifferent universe, we have the negativistic Gnostic attitude toward all materiality.

### 3. Tiny Alice

Tiny Alice, the title character, ensconced on her throne within the "model"—actually the prototype—of the castle, is queen of a kingdom at the zero point of microcosmic vanishment. She is the microcosmic equivalent to the macrocosmic God of the Christians, the model of all created things, just as He is to His believers. Also, Tiny Alice shares with the Christian God an authoritarian nature which demands abject worship and total conformity to her dictates. She, with the Christian God, is a stern ruler, setting rigid limits beyond which man may venture only at his mortal peril. These aspects are revealed in the two coincident fires on the altars—the fire in the model's chapel on the altar of Tiny Alice, and the fire in the castle's chapel on His altar—which display the wrathful response of the jealous gods to the audacity of man, the Lawyer, in going beyond the prescribed limits with his challenge that there are no limits to the possible.

Thus, with the three Alices, we find, as we found with Julian, a common Gnostic dimensionality of character. Miss Alice is the worldly manifestation of the Gnostic goddess of inner wisdom; Tiny Alice, the prototypal authority figure, equivalent to the God of the Christians whom the Gnostics recognized as the lowest members of their divine quaternity (to them he was the "Usurper God," the violator of the pre-existent unity of the acosm); and Alice, supreme etheric goddess of the seventh sphere, mediatrix between existence and the release from existence into the acosm. We thus, in the two divine aspects of the triune goddess—Tiny Alice and Alice—have the lower pair of the Gnostic quaternity. We shall encounter the two higher gods of the quaternity in the closing action.

## II. *The Proofs of the Action*

*Tiny Alice* presents in its formalized action a dramatic equivalent to a Gnostic rite. It opens with an incantation by the Cardinal that culminates in his sevenfold utterance of "do," a most apt verb whereby to describe the "doing," the creating, of his God of Creation. Apt, too, is the number seven, it symbolizing the number of spheres of existence wherein the Usurper has entrapped man. The play closes with the dying Julian crying aloud, "God, Alice...I accept thy will." The failure to capitalize the final "thy" indicates that this is no conventional obeisance to the Deity. We here encounter, with Julian's final utterance, the two lower orders of the Gnostic quaternity. As is the case with the mysteries, words cease at the pale of existence; beyond this limit words are ineffectual, and mystic action becomes the means of effecting release from the bonds of the conceivable and existent.

In the play's closing stage directions we pass this limit and encounter the two higher orders of the Gnostic quaternity in the guise of the acosmic pair, Absolute Silence and Utter Darkness. The stage directions read:

> *Julian dies.... Sounds continue thusly: thrice after the death...thump* thump *thump* thump *thump* thump. *Absolute silence for two beats.... Only when all is black...does the curtain slowly fall.*

"*Absolute silence*," "*all is black*": the divine pair of the Gnostic acosm. They are attained after a carefully detailed description of an eightfold beat, six sounding, two in silence. The eighth sphere of the Gnostics has been penetrated. Julian is annihilate.

## III. *The Proofs of the Dialogue*

Julian, in his preparation for the rite of release, had been instructed by the guardian-like admonitions of the Lawyer and Miss Alice, specifically and significantly, to surrender to "the mysteries" and to heed the "greater wisdom"—the wisdom of *gnosis*. He comes to this knowledge at the climax. Those who remain imprisoned in the coils of existence are denied this mystic knowledge. Throughout the play we have heard a recurrent refrain of frustrated confessions of ignorance. After the fire in the altars Miss Alice had said: "I don't know anything." In the final act the Lawyer, as he delivers himself of a declaration defining the limits he has come to accept, observes: "We do not know. Anything. End prologue." This does mark the end of action on the worldly plane; hereafter true action on a metaphysically transcendent level commences. It shall lead through Julian's passion and death to his acosmic apotheosis. His final words are to be an acceptance of what to Western intelligences would seem to be an impossible syncretism of faith and wisdom. With his cry, "God, Alice...I accept thy will," Julian attains *gnosis*. These we present as proofs of dialogue.

With this final proof, that of the dialogue, we close that aspect of our interpretation which contends that *Tiny Alice* is a dramatic manifestation of a Gnostic rite of acosmic release from existence. We now turn to that aspect which, we propose, demonstrates a Newtonian metaphysic.

Newton hypothesized that the fundamental element was ether. In a line of speculation that bears an uncanny resemblance to Gnostic metaphysical speculation, he advanced the theory that perhaps the whole frame of nature may be nothing but various contextures of certain etheral vapours, condensed ...and wrought into various forms, at first by the immediate hand of the Creator.... Perhaps...all things originated from ether."

The similarity between Newton's vision of God the Creator molding all things from the inceptive element of ether, and the Gnostic belief in a Usurper God similarly engaged with elemental ether, does not need underlining: the resemblance is quite apparent. And just as Newton and the Gnostics fixed upon ether as the medium by which existents might materialize from out the void, so also Albee. In an article written a year after *Tiny Alice* opened, he used an archaic and singularly unusual figure to describe the state beyond time one attains in reading or re-reading Proust; the figure, "rising etherward."

Yet the connection between Albee and Newton does not consist solely of this seemingly slender thread of verbal correspondence outside the context of the drama. We need only pursue an investigation into the ultimate nature of ether in Newton, as stated in the *Opticks*, to discover that a psychic correspondence exists between the mystic reversal of material nature Newton envisioned in etheric action, and that most perplexing between-the-acts reversal in the material nature of Miss Alice, who, after passionately embracing Julian at the close of Act II, coldly rejects him at the beginning of Act III. In E. A. Burtt's concise summary of Newton's metaphysical hypothesis, as formulated in the *Opticks*, the cause for this seemingly unmotivated change in Miss Alice is clearly evident.

> The hypothesis, in brief, is that the whole of the physical world may consist of particles which attract each other in proportion to their size, the attraction passing through a zero point into repulsion as we get down to the very minute particles that we call the ether.

"Passing through a zero point into repulsion": this is precisely the outcome of Julian's hymeneal ravishment by the
microcosmic Alice at the zero point of her castle-within-a-
castle *ad infinitum*. At the point of vanishment, attraction
changes to repulsion. With this psychic shift in the play's
symbolic figure of material nature, namely Miss Alice, at the
climax of Act II, we remain on the plane of existence. In the
culmination of Act III, when Julian in his leap of faith accepts
both the microcosmic "God" and the macrocosmic "Alice," we
reach the limit of the etheric cosmos. With the descent, according to the stage direction, of the "great presence," that which is
manifest in the absolute silence and utter darkness of the close,
we breach the leaden vault of the cosmos, transcend existence,
and attain the acosmic void.

Thus we have in *Tiny Alice* a double mystery: the Newtonian
reversal of psychic existents in Act II, and the Gnostic release
from existence in Act III. It might be asked: are these *the* two
mysteries to which Albee alluded in terming his play a "double
mystery"? There can be no certain answer, for, such is the open
nature of the creative process, no one interpretation can be
offered as final, definitive. But Albee's consciousness *did* reveal
that, for him, *Tiny Alice* is a double mystery—that he revealed,
and no more. As noted previously, after making this brief
allusion to the "double mystery," he thought better of speaking
his secret intent and sealed his lips with the terse, "I've said too
much." How Emperor Julian would have applaued his discre-
tion! He, too, had been asked to explain the mysteries, and had
responded in veiled phrases. He, too, in dealing with mystery,
turned from words to dramatic representation, writing:

> "For nature loves to hide her secrets." [Heraclitus, fragment
> 123] and she does not suffer the hidden truths about the
> essential nature of the gods to be flung in naked words to the
> ears of the profane.... Through riddles and the dramatic
> setting of myths... knowledge is insinuated into the ears of
> the multitude who cannot divine truths in the purest forms.

With *Tiny Alice*, through "riddles and the dramatic setting of myths, knowledge is insinuated into the ears of the multitude who cannot divine truths in the purest form." The mystic gift is reserved to the initiate. Perhaps if through some strange happenstance a member of the obscure sect of Gnostics which has survived in that mid-Eastern cradle of religions had chanced to be present at a performance of *Tiny Alice* he might have understood and shared his understanding of the mystic dimensions of Albee's play of mystery. We refer to the sect of whom W. Brede Kristensen wrote:

> In Southern Babylonia, the gnostic sect of Mandeans still exists, whose belief contains Babylonian, Persian, and Christian elements. According to this doctrine, man's heavenly journey proceeds upwards through the "seven prisons," the seven spheres.
>
> The journey is extensively described.... "Which prison is this, and which men does it contain?" is the question asked, and the answer given is: "Here are they who have shed blood and practiced magic."

What more might this Mandean Gnostic tell us? Much, in words. Yet, no more than Albee tells us in the "riddles and the dramatic setting of myths" of his play of double mystery, of psychic reversal and metaphysical release.

How did Albee come to do it? How did he come to follow such an alien path? Or might we not be following a false lead in raising this question? Might we not more profitably ask, is it alien? Is any path so well traveled by worshippers of the mysteries alien to us? Are we of the West so far removed from mystery that we may only now come faintly to discern it through the agency of hallucinatory stimulants? Might we not find in the release of Julian a release from the constraining bonds of Western "civilization"? Is it too late to go back, to return, with Jung, to "the likeness of that universal...man dwelling in the darkness of primordial night"? Would such a return seem shocking? Would Albee be shocked to become aware that this is the return he has effected? We feel he would not—he is prepared for the sudden gifts of the unconscious; he *knows*:

> And part of the creative act is surprising yourself. Things work from the unconscious to the conscious.

Of the truth of this we have the tangible proof of *Tiny Alice*: a maze amazing, brilliant construct of the surprising unconscious of Edward Albee.

*CINEMA*

# *Encounter with Essence:*
# *The Schematic Image*

A man's work is nothing but [a] slow trek
to rediscover, through the detours of art,
those two or three simple images in whose
presence his heart first opened.

Albert Camus[1]

Life: an opening. This the essence of encounter—the "essential encounter"—with the schematic image. Life: an opening.

We are to consider film yet I write of life. Am I off the mark? I don't think so. In Webster's, "life" is defined as "...the vital force...[of] conscious existence." Might this not, as well, be a definition of film? Apparently it would, so closely does it parallel another definition of film advanced by Robert Wagner at the 1972 conference of the University Film Association:

---

[1] Albert Camus, "The Wrong Side and the Right Side," *Lyrical and Critical*, tr. & ed. Philip Thody, (London: Hamilton, 1967).

> Film—holding in a state of permanence the fleeting image, ...closing perceptual gaps to help man discover his identity, ...[opening conceptual] ambiguities to help protean man play his role of change, [with one's] *felt* response the core.[2]

A *"felt* response" to permanence and change, to movement and image—*The Moving Image*, to use the figure that Robert Gessner of fond memory gave to his life work—which, as Sir Herbert Read has observed, has as its outcome the emergence of form from the flux of sensation: how close this is to Camus' vision of life as an opening. Film: a moving image; film: a life-form; film, its essence—an opening.

For film is a life form, a light-sensitive medium which, with all life forms, opens in its encounter with light. And film is also a symbolic form: an opening to light bodied forth in fleeting images of felt meaning we, in the race of the image, only vaguely intuit. The image is ephemeral: we see it, and it is gone.

Yet, as film critic Otis Ferguson observed: "Symbolic forms ...require...reexamination."[3] Ferguson sensed that, as Jean Cocteau noted, to see a film but once means one is likely to miss "the deep underlying design." Robert Gessner put the matter bluntly: "It is not enough to look at films; they must be studied shot-by-shot."[4] And, in the same vein, Peter Wollen had no qualms in demanding for film study the same ease of access to the screen image enjoyed by literary critics with regard to their texts, remarking that without such easy, "untrammeled" access

---

[2] Robert Wagner, "The Motion Picture in Education," paper presented at meeting of University Film Association, August 21, 1972.

[3] Otis Ferguson, *The Film Criticism of Otis Ferguson* (Philadelphia: Temple University Press, 1971), p. 32.

[4] Robert Gessner, "On Teaching Cinema in College," *Film Culture* (Winter, 1963-64), p. 48.

to film for repeated viewings, "it is very difficult to see how there can...be any significant advance in cinema study."[5]

Here, in brief, is *the* problem: how, in a one-time-only race of images lasting some five thousandths of a second, to even begin to grasp the symbolic forms and the film's underlying formal structure; how provide easy access to the film so its meanings may open to a deeper understanding?

It is encouraging to know that the problem was under consideration by the University Film Association and the American Film Institute at their spring meeting. From informal conversation with Robert Wagner, a participant, I gather that one avenue of solution being explored is the making available by industry for film study use of many more prints than presently exist of classic features. While such an estimable project can have nothing but the most earnest support, it has seemed to me that a concept enunciated in the pages of the *University Film Producers Association Journal* might be of value in assisting toward the attainment of the goal of easy access to the filmic image. Sir Arthur Elton then wrote:

> The distinguishing property of visual communication [is] not movement, but the ordered, successive presentation of images.... The elementary particle of communication, its quantum, is the static image.[6]

Elton's point, at least in my reading of it, has cataclysmic consequence to the field of film study. For does it not follow that, if the "quantum" of visual perception is "the static image," then, contrary to the traditional view, the basic unit of film is *not* the shot, but the discrete visual impact—the image?

Sir Arthur Elton's statement of this principle of visual per-

---

[5] Peter Wollen, *Signs and Meaning in the Cinema* (Bloomington: Indiana University Press, 1969), pp. 158-59.

[6] Sir Arthur Elton, "Film Considered as Language," *University Film Producers Association Journal* (No. 1, 1966), pp. 3-4.

ception is the foundation for *the* (or, at least, one) solution, I would propose, to the problem of easy access to the filmic image: sequenced still-frame.

Support for this approach is vast and varied. From the field of aesthetics—Nikolai Bukharin: an image is a "point of condensation" of experience.[7] From the field of film—Ingmar Bergman: "A film for me begins with split-second impressions";[8] Luis Bunuel: "The whole work flows from one image like a fountain"; [9] Vernon Young: "Everything in a film seems to move fluidly toward a single image that will crown...all the others...";[10] Michelangelo Antonioni: "The gradual unfolding of a picture in its fundamental images...is very important to me";[11] Sergei Eisenstein: "...the moment of culmination";[12] Robert Gessner (signally, in his book entitled *The Moving Image*): "The director first sees in his mind's eye...a still picture...a stopped frame";[13] Jean-Luc Godard: "The moment is what makes the cinema beautiful,"[14] "Cinema...seizes life."[15] And from the respective worlds of literature, psychology, and

[7] Nikolai Bukharin, in *The Problems of Aesthetics*, eds., Eliseo Vivas and Murray Krieger (New York: Rinehart, 1953), p. 501.

[8] Ingmar Bergman, *Four Screenplays*, tr. Lars Malmstrom and David Kusher (New York: Simon and Schuster, 1960), p. xv.

[9] Rayond Durgnat, *Luis Bunuel* (Berkeley: University of California Press, 1968), p. 120.

[10] Vernon Young, *Cinema Borealis* (New York: D. Lewis, 1971), p. 193.

[11] Michelangelo Antonioni, *Screenplays*, trs. Roger J. Moore and Louis Brigante (New York: Orion Press 1963), p. xiii.

[12] Sergei Eisenstein, *Film Form*, tr. Jay Leyda (Cleveland: World Publishing Company, 1949), p. 173.

[13] Robert Gessner, *The Moving Image* (New York: Dutton, 1968), pp. 84-5, 128-9.

[14] Toby Mussman, *Jean-Luc Godard, a Critical Anthology*, (New York: Dutton, 1968), p. 75.

[15] Jean-Luc Godard, in Andrew Sarris, *Interviews with Film Directors* (Indianapolis: Bobbs-Merrill, 1967), p. 214.

philosophy—Marcel Proust: "To seize...immobilize for the duration of a lightning flash...";[16] Samuel Beckett: "All that is realised in Time...a series of partial annexations...";[17] James C. Gibson: "Perception is of rigid things";[18] and Goethe: "Form is abstracted from what is in motion."[19] From the dynamic field of "still" photography (a contradiction in terms, this), Henri Cartier-Bresson: "The world is movement. I craved to seize the essence."[20] From Carl Jung: "Consciousness is a restricted field of momentary vision."[21] And, returning to the field of film aesthetics briefly, before a capping statement from Henri Bergson—Harry Alan Potamkin: "The cinema is intensive [possessing the 'intensity' of 'static motion'] as well as progressive";[22] Robert Wagner: Film "holds in a state of permanence the fleeting image...so we can look at ourselves long enough to discover our identity."[23] And finally, as noted, from Henri Bergson:

> The intellect [takes] at intervals, views that are...immobile....
> Of becoming we perceive only states....
> [We think] the moving by means of the immobile.[24]

---

[16] Marcel Proust, *The Past Recaptured*, tr., Frederick A. Blossom (New York: A. & C. Boni, 1932), p. 196.

[17] Samuel Beckett, *Proust* (New York: Grove Press, n.d.), p. 7.

[18] *The Nature and Art of Motion*, ed. Gyorgy Kepes (New York: G. Braziller, 1965).

[19] Dagobert Frey, *Gotik & Renaissance* (Augsburg: Filser, 1929).

[20] *Photographers on Photography*, ed. Nathan Lyons (Englewood Cliffs, N.J.: Prentice-Hall, 1966), pp. 42-43.

[21] C.G. Jung, *Analytical Psychology* (New York: H. Holt, 1920), p. 14.

[22] *Introduction to the Art of the Movies*, ed. Lewis Jacobs (New York: Noonday Press, 1960), pp. 165, 167.

[23] Wagner, UFA meeting, August 21, 1972.

[24] Henri Bergson, *Creative Evolution*, tr., Arthur Mitchell (Westport, Conn.. Greenwood Press, 1911, 1975).

Bergson termed this still-frame registering of motion the "cinematic mechanism of thought."

The mind is a freeze-frame printer, a cinematic mechanism, or, to bring Bergson's machine-age analogy up to date, a cinematic printout screen. William James, a contemporary of Bergson, gave attention to this process of perception and, rather than employing figuratively the motion art, cinema, to make vivid the concept of perceptual arrest in the stream of consciousness, used metaphorically the most spatially volatile life form, likening "the rhythm of thought" to the flight of a bird: brief perches at "resting places" where images are held, and "flight" which brings to the attentive mind the "relations ...between."[25] "The rhythm of thought": pause and motion. In this regard, I'm not sure if Josef von Sternberg was a reader of William James, but I am sure he was gifted with a genius for realizing this philosophic principle in his art. And we have it, the concept of Bergson and James, in a direct statement from the artist, von Sternberg having stated, "To master the laws of motion one must have the poet's insight [into] pause and rhythm."[26]

Pause and rhythm; static and kinetic; form and style. Form: static; style: kinetic—this the striking distinction drawn by Sir Herbert Read in *The Origins of Form in Art*.[27] Andrew Sarris, has, basing his view upon an aesthetic closely akin to Read's, made a sweeping claim as to the nature of film: "The art of cinema is...the style of a gesture."[28] And, with Sarris, we have Alain Robbe-Grillet on the importance of gesture: "What touches us, what persists...in memory...are the gestures."[29]

[25] William James, *Psychology* (New York: H. Holt), p. 160.

[26] Josef von Sternberg, *Fun in a Chinese Laundry* (London: Secker and Warburg, 1965), p. 325.

[27] Sir Herbert Read, *The Origins of Form in Art* (New York: Horizon Press, 1965), p. 77.

[28] Andrew Sarris, *The American Cinema* (New York: Dutton, 1968), p. 36.

[29] Alain Robbe-Grillet, *The Modern Tradition*, trs. Richard Ellmann and Charles Feidelson, Jr. (New York: Oxford University Press, 1965), p. 363.

Realizing in a vivid figure this key concept of the abstractive importance of gesture to filmic form, Bela Balazs has written in *Theory of the Film*: "The movement of the shots has the same effect as the gesturing of a narrator."[30] When we thus conceive of the scene as gesture, each image cluster of camera setups will be seen to have a structure of gestural preparation—thrust extension—and return; each scenic gesture constituting an abstractive movement-to-a-point, movement to a symbolic form. As James Joyce noted: "Gesture [renders] visible the entelechy, the structural rhythm."[31]

"Entelechy," "structural rhythm": the design of the work—this is what Joyce sought. And design is arrived at by a process of simplification, of abstraction. No artist, I suggest, is better able to speak to this point than Henri Cartier-Bresson: "At the decisive moment [there emerges] a geometric pattern..."[32] A *geometric* pattern—an abstract schema, the essence of aesthetic vision. This—an abstract schema—is what registers in the consciousness of Godard at the "extraordinary 'split' second"—"abstraction." In phenomenological aesthetics, abstractions result from one's self-world encounters. Eugene Kailin has stated the principle clearly: to be aware of form is to grasp "a schematized image."[33] While it may come as somewhat of a jolt to discover that Federico Fellini *consciously* follows a phenomenological path, discover it we did in an interview on the "Dick Cavett Show." Through some quirk in the conversational flow, talk turned to art, and Fellini remarked that "the artist sees with a schematized vision."[34] On

---

[30] Bela Balazs, *Theory of the Film*, tr., Edith Bone (New York: Dover Publications, 1953), p. 129.

[31] James Joyce, *Ulysses,* (Paris: Shakespeare and Company, 1924), p. 425.

[32] *Photographers on Photography*, ed. Nathan Lyons (Englewood Cliffs, N.J.: Prentice-Hall, 1966), pp. 47.

[33] *An Invitation to Phenomenology,* ed. James M. Edie (Chacago: Quadrangle Books, 1965), p.32.

[34] Federico Fellini, on Dick Cavett television program, January 15, 1970.

hearing this, suddenly the train of forms in Fellini's films seemed more than mere picaresque journeys (Masina's in *Cabiria*, Sordi's in *I Vitelloni*); suddenly a line from Carl Jung that I had nodded intellectual assent to, merely that, gave vivid meaning to Fellini's surrealistic vision: "The image expresses the contents of the unconscious momentarily constellated."[35] More recently, in Peter Wollen's *Signs and Meaning in the Cinema* (a phenomenological approach), we have presented us a promising lead to follow in film study. Wollen writes: the "structural," "schematic" approach discovers "motifs."[36] I can think of no more profitable pursuit for a budding filmmaker, or a fading film theorist, to engage in than the search for motifs in art, and in the work of art we, each of us, are engaged in structuring from birth to death, and beyond, far beyond, if one is of a metaphysical cast—in life. Film devotees might well continue the work so auspiciously begun by Carl Gustav Jung finding schemata in the race of image, discovering archetypal formants in the action, the Joycean entelechy, structural rhythms, the symbolic design. It may sound like a vague prospect; but, given a critically aware audience, the day when films are valued for their symbolic substance may come to pass. Jung's archetypal forms that structure the energic field of existence have been effectively applied to the study of literature; why not film? In image and sequence are to be discovered the Jungian oppositions of "light and dark, upper and lower, right and left," as well as such structuring forms as "the union of opposites in a third, the quaternity, rotation (circle and sphere), and finally a radial arrangement that usually follows some quaternity system." (Jungians will spot the latter figure as the object of mystic contemplation, the mandala.) Kenneth

---

[35] C. G. Jung, *Psychological Types*, tr. H. Godwin Baynes (London: Kegan Paul, 1923), p. 555.

[36] Peter Wollen, *Signs and Meanings in the Cinema* (Bloomington: Indiana University Press, 1972), pp. 80, 93.

Burke, in his *Rhetoric of Motives*, has pointed to ritualistic imagery patterns in dramatic action that will be found in film, as in all representational art: "the imagery of the Upward Way and the Downward Way, of...Crossing and Return, of Movement Outward and ['Movement Inward'], ...of Loosing and Binding, ['of Losing and Finding'].''[37] We round to a close, harking back to the opening superscription from Camus:

> A man's work is nothing but [a] slow trek
> to rediscover, through the detours of art,
> those two or three simple images in whose
> presence his heart first opened.

---

[37] Kenneth Burke, *A Rhetoric of Motives* (Berkeley: University of California Press, 1969), p. 535.

# The Schematized Vision of
## Josef von Sternberg in "Blonde Venus"

Josef von Sternberg, Marlene Dietrich—two names to ponder in the world of cinematic art. Their six Hollywood films have weathered changes in taste exceptionally well. While Susan Sontag's tribute to them as the highest in high camp explains one reason for their contemporary appeal, there is more reason than stylistic surface for their enduring interest. They have psychological depths that, long before Hollywood discovered Freud in the Forties, probed deeply into levels of psychic experience that only the German film of the twenties had explored.

And that brings us to our topic—the schematism that finds its roots in German film, a schematism which we find in the first Dietrich-von Sternberg film, *The Blue Angel*. After this German-made study in psychic regression, the von Sternberg-Dietrich films of the early Thirties were made in America, but they bore little resemblance to the conventional genre output of Hollywood. In style, and that's where a von Sternberg film "is at," in *style*, the von Sternberg-Dietrich films had their stylistic home in the German studios. This Germanic quality to von Sternberg-Dietrich is nowhere more clearly evident than in a 1932 production which bears a striking resemblance in German Expressionist style and motive to a German film of the same year. For in 1932 there appeared Fritz Lang's *M*, made in Germany, and von Sternberg's *Blonde Venus*, made in Hollywood: both expressionist studies of the dual nature of man, psychological studies of his mirror image, his double (Doppelgänger), his "shadow."

Yet for all the similarities between *M* and *Blonde Venus*, there is a basic difference in their thematic values: whereas *M* presents a psychic *split* ("M" itself being a symbol of duality), *Blonde Venus* presents a psychic *fusion* (Venus—Aphrodite, she born of the foam and of the sky god's male member, being a symbol of the union of the dark and light aspects of nature).

In *Blonde Venus* light and dark meet, and fuse. Such is "the schematized vision" of von Sternberg's *Blonde Venus*, "the schematized vision" of the artist. The term is Federico Fellini's. Early in the Seventies, Fellini visited the United States and was interviewed on television. In discussing his work, Fellini remarked that "the director sees with a schematized vision."

"A schematized vision": the term seemed most apt. In the race of image, as we view a film there are dominants, as in music, which give a key to the whole. And the structuring of these dominants create in one's imagination a master image, almost a geometrization, of the forces that led to the whole train of images. In the race of the image we form a schema. And when we bring an interpretation to this schematic vision, drawing upon the conventional structuring of experience of which we are cultural inheritors, we discern a meaningful order in the schema: thought and feeling crystallize in the form of a symbol. And, in approaching the work of von Sternberg, it is this symbolic aspect of the viewing, and reflecting, experience that is to be the focus of our consideration of *Blonde Venus*. We shall seek to discern the symbolic forms which structure von Sternberg's schematic vision.

That von Sternberg was an artist conscious of the formal elements of his art is evidenced in his autobiography, (*Fun in a Chinese Laundry*. London, Secker & Warburg, 1966) in which he writes feelingly of the structural elements, pause and motion: "To master the laws of motion one must have the poet's insight into pause and rhythm." And, further, he cites Goethe's ecstatic cry: "If only I could say to the moment, remain with me!" Deeply von Sternberg must have yearned for an arrest in the train of action when the symbol stands forth, revealed. How diligently he must have sought it. How well he realized these moments of brief arrest, mastering the laws of motion, and, in the stillness of the moment, shaping a patterned scheme of meaning. How well he mastered the pattern, how clear his schema, that, for the perceptive critic, there is reason to remark, as Aneas McKenzie remarked in 1936 with respect to the very "mastery of motion" of which von Sternberg was to write some thirty years later, "von Sternberg relies on elaborate shots developed by camera movement and dramatic lighting—to a point of shock, surprise, or startling beauty."

Now, before taking up the issue at hand, the symbolic values in von Sternberg's schematic points of shock, surprise, or startling beauty, first to a brief consideration of the background of the film.

*Blonde Venus* was released in the autumn of 1932, at the depth of the Depression, by Paramount. The original scenario by von Sternberg was adapted by Jules Furthman and S.K. Lauren. Cinematography was by Bert Glennon, and the design, realizing the visionary world of von Sternberg, was by Wiard Ihnen.

*Blonde Venus* was what was then popularly called a "weepie," a drama of a woman wronged who fights her way back to love and happiness. The plot, to utilize Leslie Frewin's concise synopsis, involves a cabaret singer (Helen Faraday, played by Dietrich) who, to help her seriously ill husband (Ned, Herbert Marshall), becomes a mistress of a rich man-about-town (Nick Townsend, Cary Grant). Her husband (Marshall) discovers this. She flees from city to city, first as an entertainer, finally as a prostitute. She sends her son (Johnny, little Dickie Moore) back to her husband, becomes a music hall sensation, and is happily reunited at film's end with her forgiving husband and adoring little son. A contemporary evaluation of the plot has been made by Andrew Sarris: *Blonde Venus*, Sarris writes, "exploits the sordid self-sacrifice which movies of this era prescribed for its female stars. They paraded down Sin Street, usually more sinned against than sinning, for the sake of home and hearth." However, although *Blonde Venus*, from a critical viewpoint, may have been viewed as a "weepie," the sentimental recording of a woman's fall and regeneration, von Sternberg viewed it differently, noting that it was "based on a story" he had "written swiftly to provide something other than the sob stories that were being submitted." Von Sternberg's intention, then, was to produce "something other than" a sentimental romance-melodrama. We have a hint as to what he might have had in mind from a comment he made on writing *Blonde Venus*: "I became more and more partial to fancy." And the production was to realize this intent: the baroque extravagance that was to culminate in *The Devil Is a Woman* (1935) is a pronounced feature of *Blonde Venus*.

One of the main reasons that *Blonde Venus* appeals to me, personally, is its use of an exotic American rather than foreign locale. It is this haunting atmosphere of a decadent Southland that appeals, as well, to Curtis Harrington. In Harrington's view, the low world of *Blonde Venus*, with its "low dives, its [sleazy] nightclubs, its [seedy] hotel rooms, its flophouses," was to become "the archetype" of the distinct genre of Hollywood gangster and private-eye B-movies of the Thirties and

Forties. And, closer to the present, this subterranean world of Gulf and Tidewater coasts which von Sternberg explored is akin to the world we find, some forty years later, in Dennis Hopper's *Easy Rider* (1969).

We might also note that, in addition to this quality of recognition that we find in the environmental atmosphere of *Blonde Venus*, there is a contemporary quality to the way it is handled—with an offhand arbitrariness. Andrew Sarris observes that "Dietrich's nightclub numbers are utterly unmotivated in terms of plot," and finds in this "a key to the extreme stylization of Dietrich's character, extreme even for von Sternberg." In this connection, one "stylized" *outré* sequence that has received almost universal recognition is the image of the Divine Marlene in her nightclub gorilla suit. *Time*, in its review in 1932, noted, "Good shot: a fake cabaret gorilla rocking formidably from side to side, pulling off one paw to expose a slender white hand (Dietrich's)." This image of goddess-as-beast marked in John Kobal's view, "a high watermark in camp—Dietrich's 'Hot Voodoo' number." Susan Sontag, in her "Notes on Camp," has also commented on this campiest of "Camp" scenes: "Camp is the outrageous aestheticism of Sternberg's six American movies with Dietrich."

But appreciation of the bizarre only touches the periphery of the significance of this androgynous vision. Venus emerged from her grotesque casing as Aphrodite, sprung from the male member of the god, stepped from the foam. This interest in the androgyne von Sternberg shares with another artist of exotic *tendance*, Baudelaire. And this allusion to depths unexplored brings us to the central matter—the archetypal imagery in von Sternberg's schematized tracing of the mythic journey of eternal return.

"No search is made unless one is vague," said Josef von Sternberg. This statement by an artist who followed the way of intuition reveals an awareness of the unconscious source of creative form. Von Sternberg gave further indication of this awareness in a letter in 1960 and an interview in *Positif* in 1961, having then stated: "We are influenced by everything: these walls, this room.... And influence often comes from within. [Man], with his [complex] heritage, is influenced in the main by as yet unlisted factors." Later von Sternberg noted: "As I get older, ...I study anthropology and psychiatry." It is interesting that Jean-Luc Godard began with a study of ethnology, while this interest in man's cultural heritage became an ever-greater interest to von Sternberg. From his use of mythic subject-matter in much of his work, it is apparent that this cultural interest was a long and continuing one: indeed, he used a mythic source for the title of *Blonde Venus*. As he wrote the opening action he might well have had the Venus myth in mind, for in the opening scene Helen describes how she was discovered by the young medical student at her bath in the pond, an action which has a resonance of the birth of the golden goddess, Aphrodite, rising from the foam. Further, possible subtle allusion to the foam-born nature of Venus is to be found in the dialogue at the opening between mother and son. As she bathes him, Johnny says: "Look Mommy, I'm a fish," to which she replies, "I thought you were a boat." We recall that Venus Astarte had a son, Ichthys, a name relating to the piscine world.

Applying the "schematized vision" of the artist, as framed by Fellini, if we were to schematize the fish we would find a mandorla, a spindle form. Two curved lines intersect, making an almond-shaped figure. This mandorla form, as Maurice Schneider points out, symbolizes the spinning out of the thread of life, as in the lunar cycle. We recall that the spindle shape is related to the moon's three-phased emergence and recession, and that the moon goddess is triform, as are the three Fates, who spin, measure, and cut the thread of existence. The spindle, the fish—mandorla shapes—symbolize the intersection of the spheres, of the upper and lower worlds. It is the symbol of inversion, of psychic exchanges between the dual energies of ascent and descent. These energies symbolized in the dual curves of the upward and downward arcs meet in the spindle and piscine mandorla form of the Magna Mater, herself a manifestation of the invisionary process.

There are three visualizations of the mandorla figure of inversion in *Blonde Venus*: one in the hotel room in Chattanooga to which Helen flees with her small son; another at the depths of her despair, after she has given up her son to his father, in the hostel for derelicts in Galveston; and a final instance of symbolic inversion in the scene of reconciliation in the New York apartment when the family is reunited. Let us take them up in order: first, the scene in the hotel room in Chattanooga.

After having been charged with vagrancy and ordered out of town, Helen is discovered in the hotel room where she has hurried to get her small son. We pan right with her as she approaches the bed upon which he is asleep. As we pan right the iron bedstead's tendril-like curvilinear whorl-forms appear in the foreground. They are made up of two large circles flanking a central motif—a vertical mandorla which is dissected by a central vertical rod. She stops, frame center, her figure dissected by the vertical rod of the mandorla. She bends down to her small son and picks him up, his figure, once again, symmetrically encompassed by and divided by the mandorla and its central vertical rail. At this point what can only be interpreted as a deliberately designed optical effect takes place: the screen darkens at the top and bottom of the frame in a vertical wipe. The wipe holds in a narrow horizontal slit, before obscuring the scene. Discernible in this narrow horizontal format is the undulant line of the bedstead's lower rail and the triform convergent arrow-form of the lower half of the mandorla and its vertical member. The arrow points down, an omen of the descent Helen is shortly to undergo in her descent to the lower depths in the Gulf Coast town of Galveston. The arrow points down—to the undulant rise in the wave-like swell of the bedstead's lower rail. Again, the symbol is meaningful in the context of the dramatic action: Helen, we are to find, is, figuratively, to experience a rite of purification in the waters—but of this image of rebirth in the waters we shall defer comment till the next sequence in Galveston, of which it forms the capping image.

After giving up her son in a poignantly moving scene at the railroad station—a sequence which has as its culminating image a vision in long shot of Helen (Dietrich) in profile, standing forlorn on the tracks gazing tearfully after the receding train, with, again, a symbol auguring her eventual regeneration in the healing waters: she trails a long scarf of tulle, its lightness wafted by the breeze stirred in the wake of the departing train which carries her child from her, its gently undulant action echoing the poignant surge of her desolate desire, forming a wave of grief engulfing her—after this scene of desolate isolation we follow Helen in her descent to the depths of her despondency in the Galveston flophouse.

We pan right once more with her movement. She stops to talk to another down-and-outer, who huskily speaks of suicide. Helen too would end it all, would commit suicide by drowning, "making," as she puts it, "a hole in the water." As she speaks she engages in a remarkable bit of mime that counters the tenor of her words: she grasps a rope which hangs from the ceiling and jauntily—there is no other word, I feel, to describe her action—jauntily swings back and forth as she answers the gruff question of her companion in distress, "Why are you going to kick off?" with a cavalier, "Because that's the way I feel; isn't that reason enough?" There is a dual edge to her words and their countering mime accompaniment. There has also been a hint of inversion in her choice of the striking figure "to make a hole in the water" to describe her despondent state: the figure of the hole symbolizes both destruction and creation, just as the action of immersion relates to both death and annihilation and to rebirth and regeneration. Additionally, the act of hanging has dual erotic significance, connoting both the positive and negative aspects of intercourse: castration and sexual fulfillment. Further, there is a subtle mythic equivalence in her act of hanging: another Helen, Helen Dendrites, the Greek tree goddess, in one version of the Trojan myth, suffered death by hanging for the havoc she wrought on the Greek cause.

That von Sternberg was aware of such mythic correspondences to Greek myth in his work is evident from the title he originally intended for his autobiography, *A Guide to the Labyrinth*. In the labyrinthine depths lurked the fabled beast, the Cretan Minotaur, symbol of the regressive attraction of the abyss. Helen, in her descent into the depths of depravity, faces the abyss, and faces it down. She chooses life. Triumphantly asserting, "I am the Queen of Hearts," she begins her climb from the slough of despond; we follow her as she retraces her steps out of this scene of dereliction and, in a long dissolve, encounters the agent of her regeneration, the waters—we hold on a wide expanse of ocean, its rippled back-lit surface a stream of light to the far horizon.

There follows the cursorily handled sequence of her triumph in a Parisian revue and her decision, on Nick's (Cary Grant's) prompting, to return to her husband (Herbert Marshall) and child—if they will have her.

Von Sternberg's handling of the scene of reconciliation is remarkable for its unbelievably audacious symbolism: he manages to so structure Helen's (Dietrich's) costume that the symbol of inversion, the mandorla, is unmistakably present. Helen, having been accepted back by Ned, resumes her domestic chores. She is hardly dressed for them: removing her wrap we see that she is encased in a very revealing black sheath. The décolletage is extreme, and beneath its deep plunging cleft is—a mandorla: the fabric so cut as to reveal a mandorla-shaped bare midriff. The symbolic wonder of her costume does not cease here: she turns her back to Ned (and to us) as she goes to the kitchen. Revealed is the very low slashed-V of the back-line of her dress; exposed, the white of her back and the gentle curve of her bare shoulders. Her torso forms yet one more mandorla. Von Sternberg's sly ingenuity is not exhausted with this marvel of symbolic costuming: he manages to insinuate yet one more mandorla, this time through an object Helen carries from the kitchen—on a motherly errand to nourish her son, she bears in her hands a plate. Its shape the ellipse, its symbolic value the inversionary process which has informed each crucial scene of *Blonde Venus*.

From the depths Helen has risen, triumphant. This scene of feminine ascendancy brings to mind a poem seen written in bold letters on a mirror before which Helen, in her mannish tuxedo—"the illusion of perfect indifference" (Dietrich, as seen by Leslie Frewin)—has sung "I Couldn't Be Annoyed." Triumphant Helen, at the peak of her career in her Paris revue, staring down the world, backed by the blazoned declaration of her ethos (and Rudyard Kipling's):

> Down to Gehenna,
> Up to the throne,
> He travels furthest
> Who travels
> ALONE!

—the Blonde Venus.

The journey we have traced of her fall and rise, her descent into the depths and her ascent to worldly fame, does not begin to measure the ground we have covered. Surely, in light of the intricately devised symbology that accents each turn in the dramatic action, the Blonde Venus's "furthest" journey— *alone*—is not to be found in the ostensible plot. Her (and von Sternberg's) furthest journey—for as von Sternberg, Flaubert-like, was to confess in a *Cahiers* interview in 1965, "You must remember that in my films Marlene is not herself.... I am Marlene..."—rather *their* "furthest" journey has been into the realm of forms, archetypal forms. In *Blonde Venus* Dietrich and von Sternberg ventured to the furthest reaches of schematic vision.

The director sees with a schematized vision.

As we began with this aperçu of Fellini, so we close with it. The formal imagery of *Blonde Venus*, as envisioned by Josef von Sternberg, gives graphic definition to an abstract form—the archetype of fused duality, of psychic wholeness: the mandorla, the flying shuttle of Moira, of the triform goddess. *Blonde Venus*, rising from the deep waters of the subconscious, as had her namesake, Aphrodite, she born-of-the-foam, offers a moving vision of the healing of the agonizing dichotomy that underlies existence. *Blonde Venus*, in its gossamer web—and it is not mere idle fancy that led von Sternberg to utilize, as a recurrent musical motif, Mendelssohn's incidental music to *A Midsummer Night's Dream*—presents us with a precious psychic gift: a schematic vision of the healing, through mystic grace, of the wound of Being.

# *Fritz Lang's "M":*
# *Symbol of Transformation*

...what passes in my subconscious;
it is for you to discover...
Fritz Lang
(in *Luc-Mollet*)

Fritz Lang here hints at depths to be explored.

Many of Lang's works invite depth analysis: the Mabuse sequence, *Metropolis*, *M*.

*M*—its very title is an invitation to archetypal study. And, upon close examination, this promise is fulfilled: a deep symbolic significance is discoverable in every production aspect in its title graphics, its dramatic action, settings, staging, camera action, and musical motif.

That Lang and writer Thea von Harbou should subconsciously have created this manifold pattern of symbolic forms is difficult to credit. Surely, as they selected the title graphic, an

open palm bearing an "M" brand, they might well have been
aware of the subtle trace their image bore of the mystic vision
of Rainer Maria Rilke's soaring descent:

> But up in the southern sky, pure as within the palm
> of a consecrated hand, the clearly-resplendent *M*,
> standing for Mothers...[1]

> Aber im südlichen Himmel, rein wie im Innern
> einer gesegneten Hand, das klar erglänzende *M*,
> das die Mütter bedeutet...

We are to find "the Mothers" at the close of *M*. Their light is
then to be of an order other than beneficent.

The film opens with Elsie, soon to be Kürten's third victim,
standing, immobile, in the center of a ring of seven children.
They circle her in a counterclockwise direction. Elsie is the pole
of this encircling vernal rite of death.

Since, in this reading of the action, the film presents a
process of psychic transformation, the studies of C.G. Jung are
central in seeking to interpret the symbolic values which
inform nearly every scene. This opening image repays reference
to Jungian studies. Jung, in *Symbols of Transformation*, leads
us to a relevant alchemical formula: "At the pole lies the heart
of Mercury," the god of transformation.[2] In *Psychology of the
Transference* Jung has elaborated upon this protean god's
transformational function: "Mercury...symbolizes the unconscious.... In one way it is a...monster, but in another sense it is
the 'philosopher's child.' "[3]

---

[1] Rainer Maria Rilke, *Duino Elegies* X, trs, J.B. Leishman and Stephen
Spender (New York: W.W. Norton, 1939).

[2] C.G. Jung, *Symbols of Transformation*, tr. R.F.C. Hull (Princeton, N.J.:
Princeton University Press, 1956).

[3] C.G. Jung, *Psychology of the Transference*, tr. R.F.C. Hull (Princeton,
N.J.: Princeton University Press, 1954).

Mercury-M, pursuer-pursued, assailant-victim: the mystic *coincidentia oppositorum* which informs the Oedipal myth.

Elsie's brief dalliance with the stranger begins at noon. Jung has noted in *Modern Man in Search of a Soul*: "At the stroke of noon the descent begins."[4] Numerologically, adding the digits, the meeting of opposites commences under the fateful number, three. We recall that Oedipus killed Laius "where three roads meet," at the point where the triform goddess, Hecate, in her crone aspect, exercised her malevolent powers.

Elsie's mother steps out onto the stairwell landing and peers down. We see a labyrinth of receding stairs and railings. Descent now is underway into the lair of the Minotaur. In myth, the labyrinth could also take the form of a sinister forest. As we gaze down the stairwell, Kürten is luring Elsie into such a trap—and, in an Oedipal perspective, who is not to say that Kürten, as well, is himself a victim of entrapment?

Elsie is next seen approaching a kiosk upon which is posted "*Wer ist der Mürderer?*" The ball with which she is playing rises into the frame three times. A shadow profile of Kürten moves into the frame, blocking out all but the "M" in *Murderer*. We hear the whistled strains of "In the Hall of the Mountain King." It is heard each time Kürten falls prey to his blood lust. The melody is an odd choice for its atmospheric function. Admittedly, it has about it a degree of menace in its stalking melodic line, and its obsessive repetiveness was enough to drive Grieg to remark "I can tolerate it no longer!" But this only begins to explain why Lang chose to employ it. We recall that "M" is a symbol for the mountain of Janus, the god of duality. "In the Hall of the Mountain King" constitutes yet one more instance of dualistic conjunction: "hall" is a feminine symbol; "mountain" and "king," masculine. And, again, its melodic line describes an "M." Further, there is an unmistakable duality to

---

[4] C.G. Jung, *Modern Man in Search of a Soul*, trs. W.S. Dell and Cary F. Baynes (New York: Harcourt, Brace & World, 1968).

the announcement of an upcoming concert beneath the "wanted" notice: "Kurt Klawitzsky, Feb. 11th," the "K," the 11th letter, and the 11th day of the second month all being numerologically reducible to "two."

Kürten and Elsie proceed to the balloon vendor where he buys her a balloon in the form of a puppet which, in its bulbous head and torso and loosely dangling legs, again forms the recurring image, "M." And above the vendor a "K"—the eleventh letter, symbolic of duality—is revealed on a sign, the rest of the wording being obscured by the display of balloons.

A cutaway to a wide shot of a darkened laundry room in Elsie's apartment house, suggesting, in its emptiness, the missing child, reveals a dress upon a clothesline, its arms dangling in such a manner that they and the neck-line of the low bodice describe an "M."

By indirect set-ups Lang next subtly reveals the fate of Elsie: the ball is seen rolling to a stop upon a pine-needled forest floor, and the balloon puppet is seen breaking free of its entanglement in the telephone wires and, borne by the wind, sinuously weaving out of the frame.

The murder now a matter of public knowledge and concern, panic infests the city. A gentleman is pulled by a well-dressed mob from an omnibus. On the railing is a poster for "PK Kaugumm." The framing is precise: only the "K" in a white circle is revealed.

The police are now seen swinging into action. The candy bag found at the scene of the crime is shown us, so crumpled as to form an "M." A compass scribes a third circle on a map of the city: "Every day we enlarge the circle." Significance attaches here: we are to find the fateful number three to be the symbol of Kürten's nemesis.

Kürten is next seen before a mirror in his apartment, closely studying his features. He presses his second fingers to the corner of his mouth. They describe two fangs.

It is announced that three Aristo cigarettes have been found near the murder scene; the fateful three—nemesis approaches.

The underworld then assembles to plan strategies to apprehend the criminal and restore "order." A pickpocket, awaiting the arrival of their black-gloved leader, displays his pelf: three watches. At three o'clock the leader arrives. Time has begun to run out on Kürten: at the third hour of the third day after his third murder.

Now commences an intricate series of actions on the street as Kürten hunts a fourth victim.

At a toy shop two women hurriedly shepherd two children off. In the window is a protective talisman, a rotating Meccano Seal-of-Solomon, also known in cabbalistic circles as the Shield of Moses: the transcendent pentacle, two interlaced triangles. Support for this reading of the scene is found in the frame: in the lower left corner a shadowy figure can be made out—a kneeling mendicant with a long patriarchal beard.

In a long shot Kürten is next seen scanning a display of cutlery. On the wall beside the show window is the trademark of the Haenkel Twinwerke, the stick-figure twins; their middle legs are joined in such a way that their lower members describe an "M."

A reverse-cut reveals Kürten; tattooed across his face are reflected the rows of knives in the window display. They describe a streaked band of serrated light—savagely primitive. A subjective close up then discloses the object of his rapt attention: a semi-circular display of glistening spoons—the opening of the cave, seat of the mysteries. We then cut-back to Kürten, its cyclic reflection at his waist. This is followed by another subjective close up of the rhomboid band of knives and the mirror it frames. Reflected within its serrated flames we see a young girl. She is standing with her hands resting on a hip-high railing of a most singular construction: its three vertical members form yet another "M," symbol of duality. Behind her a heavy truck wheel's spokes form about her head a spiked aureole. A circle with radial lines symbolizes woman, the rose, and, in the East, the transcendent flower, the lotus.

Kürten feels the corner of his mouth, echoing the gesture

which earlier, in his room, had given him a lupine countenance.

The child moves out of sight. Kürten follows with snake-like stealth.

Next, the whorl of chaos figure is encountered in an optician's window. Beside it a large cardboard arrow, pointed earthward, with a bulbous protuberance on its shaft, rises and falls. The arrow and the circle: male and female fusion. Once more we encounter the fused duality.

A young girl crosses the frame. Kürten backs furtively into a doorway. The child runs to a woman: "Oh, Mother...I wanted to meet you halfway!" In the bookstore behind the embracing mother and child is framed a picture suggestive of a Rorschach split image. Beneath it, in the darkness, three vertical bars of dotted light are reflected: the Scorpio form of "M"—symbol of unbridled sensuality.

The mother and child leave the frame. We hold on Kürten. The helix of chaos spins behind him; the arrow rises and falls, its shadow having shifted so it now falls on the chaos figure, penetrating its center. To the alchemists, opposition of the arrow (male) and the whorl form (female) represented a mystic transformation. Further, in Classic antiquity, the contracting whirlpool symbolized the feminine lunar force of regression that would pull man back and down. It is akin to Charybdis, the devouring sea-goddess who thrice daily exacted human sacrifice. Kürten, too, meted out a threefold fatal toll.

Kürten is next seen to enter a trellised beer-garden. The undulant shape of the awning forms an "M," while another series of "M" forms are created by the decorative woodwork of the wall panelling. Through the heavy growth of the Dionysiac vine, we observe Kürten press his hands to his ears to stop the rising-falling line of the Pan-like piping that would lead him to fall prey to his lust.

From Kürten we then shift to the sightless balloon vendor. He hears Kürten's whistle and calls a nearby ruffian, one of the army of beggars and petty thieves the underground has rallied to ferret out the murderer. The vendor and his cohort are situated in an area undergoing street repair. They are flanked by two parallel poles supported by saw-horses: "XX." Additionally, the strings of the balloons tugging on the blind man's right hand, as they cross, form "XX," the "M" below, its mirror image, "W," above. We well might contemplate in this context the symbolic import of the thrusts of their respective central angles; whereas "M" marks descent, "W" heralds ascent.

Significantly, in addition to the ever-present symbol of duality, there is a new symbolic power visible in the key scene: the symbol of the unity—the obelisk.

Here we have the first schematic image of reversal of earthbound force. Here, as in the Egyptian pyramid, we have the mystic symbol of the triumph of life over death. This is the point of *peripeteia*, of dramatic reversal, as the blind man, backed by the obelisk, points his finger accusingly toward the killer. Kürten's fortune changes: hunter now becomes the hunted.

One further aspect of symbolic valence occurs in this scene at the turning point in the action: the camera, as it moves in upon the blind vendor at his moment of recognition (*anagnorisis*), veers right, left, right, left in following the vendor's accomplice as he begins to trail Kürten, the camera movement thus describing an "M."

We next move to a cellar candy shop. Its semi-circular double window forms an M-form. Kürten buys the child an ice cream cone: schematized, it constitutes an inverted arrow and an orb, a three-dimensional realization of the cardboard arrow in the optician's.

Kürten, upon emerging from the shop, is discovered to have purchased an apple. He draws his knife; its blade, point downward, catches the light in a blinding flash. He then carefully cuts a quarter section, leaving an "M" shape.

The underworld minion who is trailing Kürten then is observed to take a piece of chalk and inscribe an "M" upon his open palm. Following this we see him jostle Kürten in passing, striking him upon the back of his left shoulder. We then cut-in to the knife lying upon a drain in the cobblestone street, it having been knocked out of Kürten's hand. Its blade points downward, with a rhomboid drain nearby. This diamond shape we recall from the mirror in which Kürten spotted his fourth intended victim. Then the rhomboid of knives of the mirror's frame had vibrated, the male force was then vital; now there is symbolized in knife and drain Kürten's descent.

The child retrieves the knife and proffers it to the still startled Kürten. He takes it haltingly, and slowly turns away, exposing upon his back the fateful brand—"M."

There is mystic significance in the manner in which the brand was applied. Goblet D'Alviella notes that the open left hand symbolizes the "Chaldean Cylinder."[5] The Chaldeans, a Middle-Eastern sect of Semitic gnostics, followed the way of the mysteries. To them the open palm signified the "Hand of Justice." They imprinted it upon their thresholds to guard against evil. Yet further symbolic value attaches to the open palm: "K," the eleventh letter of the Hebraic alphabet, derives from "the hollow of the hand."

At yet another toy shop we find a Lotte Reiniger-like marionette, its legs scissoring spasmodically. Since Kürten is positioned directly beneath it, its legs figuratively decapitate him in yet another symbolic representation of his loss of power.

We move to an adjoining window of the toy shop featuring a display of dominoes, preparatory to his unmasking when his persona will be stripped away exposing shadow to view. Kürten sees himself in a mirror. He spots the brand. Terror grips him. The child attempts to erase the mark. Kürten wheels around. We reverse angle to catch a glimpse of the shadowy figure who had branded him dodging behind a truck. Kürten's game is up. He takes flight.

---

[5] Goblet D'Alviella, *The Migration of Symbols* (London: A. Constable, 1894).

The underground moves in upon Kürten's hiding place in a State Bank building storeroom at eleven o'clock, after a three-hour delay while waiting for the propitious moment for their raid. Kürten finds himself trapped; the lockerroom door is locked. Frantic, he attempts to pry open the lock with his knife. The blade breaks, in yet another symbolic emasculation.

The underground captures Kürten with three minutes to go before the police are to arrive on the scene. Kürten is stuffed in a sack, in a return-to-the-womb equivalent, however grisly, and dragged off to a catacomb-like room in a deserted distillery. A kangaroo court has assembled. He is dragged down a flight of steps and then thrown down before the court; he rises and strives to escape, fleeing back up the steps, only to be thrown down once more. The figure described in the staging action: "M."

The low-ceilinged room confronts us with classic frontality; two brick pillars and side arches describe an "M," and long plank tables upon trestles describe yet another.

Teiresias-like, the blind balloon vendor identifies the murderer, his sinister hand falling upon Kürten's shoulder in an echo of the branding gesture.

Culprit now formally charged, the trial commences. Kürten pleads, "Always I feel someone behind me, pursuing me...my other self...soundlessly." An old man nods assent. All share guilt. We are put in mind of Hermann Hesse's *Steppenwolf*, published but two years before *M* was released in 1931: "The judge who sits over the murderer...recognizes all the emotions and potentialities of the murderer in his own soul and hears the murderer's voice as his own."[6]

And, deep within, do we not, as well, recognize the Oedipal cry of terror in Kürten's cry: "Ghosts of fire hover over me— there is no escape!"? He, man exposed, is engulfed in the arrow forms that burn in the northern sky, fierce counterpart to the

---

[6] Hermann Hesse, *Steppenwolf*, tr. Basil Creighton (New York: H. Holt & Company, 1929).

serrate splendor of the southern sky apostrophized in Rilke's closing Duino Elegy. And that the personage hiding behind the flames is the devouring goddess is not long hidden from us as the vengeful action closes on its victim.

A public defender steps forth from the crowd. His argument: compulsion relieves one of responsibility. The prosecutor, black-handed, counters: "If he must murder, then he must be exterminated."

Defender: "The state does not have the right, nor do you."

Prosecutor: "Ask the mothers!"

A woman: "Kill him! Beast!"

A ghastly light is cast on "the shadow" which Jolande Jacobi describes as falling "on the threshold of the realm of the 'Mothers.' "

At the climax of their rage the crowd begins to move in upon the tragic scapegoat. He cringes in foetal contraction. The defender cries: "I demand this man be given the protection of the law!" A police whistle is heard. All freeze. They raise their hands. A right hand enters the frame and grasps Kürten's shoulder, the third hand to so touch him. "In the name of the Law." Thus ends the film—deliverance.

Yet is there deliverance in this world, in our time? As the end title comes on the screen, the open palm bearing the brand of "M," we might ponder: does it symbolize a spiritual deliverance or an atavistic regression? This, the enigma we all carry in our cupped palm: this, the intimate symbol of transformation—"M."

# The "Heights of Abstraction" in Antonioni: "L'Avventura"

> Man...is under the sway of forces
> and myths...the same as...pre-
> vailed at the time of Homer.
> Michelangelo Antonioni

*L'Avventura* (1960) is a perplexing masterpiece. It goes far beyond the conventional commercially circumscribed range of film, touching levels of metaphysical extension only gnostics might sense, and yet it suffers a failure of nerve in the closing action that drops it from these cosmic reaches to the shallow sink of sentiment. I should prefer to look away from its ending—the scene of "reciprocated pity" on the piazza as Claudia forgives Sandro for being a man—and look to its metaphysical perspectives. They are impressive. Though Antonioni is no philosopher in the formal sense, he is one most assuredly in the abstract working out of his creative subconscious. His is "...a dream all charged with symmetries..."[1]

---

[1] Paul Valery, "Dance of the Soul."

There are symmetries in *L'Avventura's* imagery from first
frame to last; if one credits Antonioni's remark (in the *Screenplays,* New York, 1963) that *L'Avventura* is "a mystery in
reverse," one might expect revelation in the opening sequence.
Such is the case.

We open on a young brunette, Anna (Lea Massari), striding
toward us through a stone arch, along a stone wall, and,
turning right in an approach, bringing us a gesture of revelation: as she passes through the combined shade of nearby pines
and reflected sunlight from a window of the villa flanking the
path, the effect of Anna's passage through the extremes of light
and dark—the left side of her face illuminated by the reflected
glare of the sun; then passing into deep shade, to emerge once
more into the light of the sun, the right side of her face struck by
its harsh direct rays—is to present us, in effect, with the three
phases of the moon: the old crescent, the dark face, and the
new. Anna, figuratively, has experienced transformation,
inversion. And that the young lady's name is "Anna" is apt,
Anna being a Janus-like palindrome. Further, there is subtle
numerological symbology in her name, of which more later,
when we shall consider the strange correspondence existing
between the film's modern saga set in the Liparian and Aeolian
Islands and in Sicily and the mystic philosopher Pythagoras of
Kroton, Sicily.

We note the tree under which Anna walks at this opening
shot of Antonioni's great trilogy is the pine. It is worthy of
remark that this tree is to form the backdrop for the last shot of
Monica Vitti—the vital life force of Antonioni's trilogy—in the
third and concluding section, *L'Eclisse* (*Eclipse*, 1962). There is
mythic reference to be discerned here: the pine of Attis,
"yclypt," the castrated god. Contrariwise, when note is taken of
the instrumentation of Giovanni Fusco's Spartan musical
arrangement in this passage, as in the whole score—wind
instruments, with an emphasis on the most sylvan of the winds,
the clarinet—the pipes of Pan might be sensed in the air, for

Pan loved a wood nymph, Pitys, who, fleeing from his advances, turned into a pine. When it is realized that this vital young maid is to flee from her lover, the correspondence is clear. Also, along the same mythic line, we recall that another of Pan's loves, Syrinx, evading his ardor, turned into a bed of reeds from which Pan fashioned his pipe.

That the blonde protagonist, Claudia, who inherits the central dramatic locus upon the disappearance of her dark friend, Anna, also is party to this mythic reference shall become evident in the dialogue of her flirtation with Sandro toward the end of the film. Then Claudia is to playfully chide him: "Before you leave...tell me that when you leave without me it's as if you had only one leg.... You'll limp." This puts one in mind of the crippled smithy god, Hephaestus, who, with many Greek gods, came to be connected with his Roman equivalent, Vulcan, god of the forge. And we should not forget, Hephaestus'-Vulcan's forge was in the volcanic Lipari Islands—the setting for the search sequence of *L'Avventura*. And Claudia then goes on to make yet one more mythic allusion: "You must tell me that you want to kiss my shadow on the walls." Pan, as noted, had loved wraiths which vanished as he reached out to them and found in their stead Syrinx, the reed, and Pitys, the pine.

Again, relating to Pythagoras, the Greek philosopher of mystic provenance who worshipped the god of order, Apollo, we recall that Apollo loved Daphne, who, as he sought to embrace the nymph, turned into a tree bearing her name.

Additionally, Hephaestus-Sandro finds further mythic correspondence in the nature of the smithy god's birth and upbringing: lame from birth, Hephaestus was thrown from Olympus by his mother, who, Athena-like, bore him alone. As he fell, two sea goddesses (Anna and Claudia?) caught him and sheltered him in their sea grotto for nine years. Three, nine...is a sequence sacred to the moon goddess, the symbol of inversion.

And that fact might well be kept in mind when, shortly after this opening action of Anna's encounter with her father, she has a tryst with Sandro in his apartment while, below, Claudia waits. We see Claudia through the narrow opening in the window drapes. The railing is of intertwined circles, each circle overlapping the one next to it, making almond-shaped mandorlas. And, center-screen, we see such a mandorla—symbol of the meeting of opposites, as at the rising and setting of sun and moon when their orbs are cut by the horizon.

Mention of the sun, moon, and earth brings us to consider a very strange conjunction of elemental forces in the Island sequence when water-air and earth-water are encountered in two sequent scenes.

First, in a very striking image, we discover a water spout rising from the sea. Next we see, over Claudia's shoulder, a large boulder plummetting into the water. Claudia contemplates its watery disturbance, then is attracted to a distant figure. Rising, her hands press the earth, fingers splayed, as she cries out, "Anna!" I cannot help seeing this conjunction of "Anna" with the dactyls as symbolically significant, for the name, I feel, describes numerologically the metaphysic of existence: A-N-N-A, 1-5-5-1 is a mystic diagram of the five elements' creation and cancellation. In the *mise-en-scène* we have just had figured the conjuntion of opposites: the skyborne waters of the tornado; the watery grave of the stone. Only fire has seemingly been absent; yet it is ever present in the Liparian Islands. The very earth is fire-born, volcanic in origin. We recall the delight with which the venturers encountered the symmetric cone of a distant island silhouetted against the shining sea. Further, central to A-N-N-A, we have the quintessence, the fifth essence that goes beyond existence. She, beside the shore of the island ominously named Lisca Bianca (White Fish), had met a black shark—in her fancy, to be sure, but are not things imagined more real that those encountered in actuality?

And what, the skeptical reader might ask, would Antonioni make of all this reading into, and beyond, his images? In reply I would cite his acceptance of an interpretation of the closing scene by noted film historian Georges Sadoul: "The frame [of the scene of tearful reconciliation at dawn on the piazza] is divided exactly.... On the one side...Etna...snowy; on the other...a concrete wall." Antonioni interpreted this to be symmetric dividing of the psychological nature of his two protagonists. The woman, Antonioni identified with the distant snowy peak of the fire cone, and man, with the blank stone face of the wall. This interpretation is possible. I should offer another. For this brings us to my opening remark on the failure of nerve that *L'Avventura* suffers, in my judgment, in its closing action. I would rather it end on a metaphysical level. And Antonioni might so have ended it, for, citing Lucretius, he had observed, "The only thing certain is the existence of a secret violence..." —a violence expressive of a secret order, a Pythagorean order, as that discoverable in the harmonics of Apollo's lyre.

It relates to the score Fusco wrote in reponse to Antonioni's request for a jazz score in the "Hellenic" mode. In this regard, we might take into account Paul Valéry's remark on his poem, "Le Cimitiere Marin," that it "began in me by a rhythm of... four and six." The rhythm, and title, find a concurrence in *L'Avventura*; upon encountering the deserted village, Claudia is to remark, "It's not a town. It's a cemetary." (It also bears noting that Valéry's sentimental observation that "at the basis of every thought is a sigh" finds a resonance in Antonioni's ending in "mutual pity.")

Fusco's opening theme features a leaping dance-like figure of two pointed-note rising triads to a four-beat rhythm. It is tonically suggestive of the tragic dithyramb.

The music at the close is to be discordant, ending on a sustained unresolved chord. Standing over Sandro, Claudia is the feminine "life force"—Etna, a fire cone encased in a frigid mantle. Seated, Sandro has, Attis-like, been unmanned. At the opening Anna, aquatic, ventured and sought oblivion. At the close, Sandro is bound in lithic immobility.

The opening line of dialogue, heard off-screen as Anna

approached the speaker, a minion of her wealthy father, is prescient: "They'll suffocate this poor villa of yours." It finds an echo in the closing action wherein a guilt-ridden male is literally "suffocated" by the moral strictures of the Church in whose ruins we come to the pathetic close.

At the opening Anna's gesture had been one of spiteful cancellation; she, the maelstrom.

At the close Claudia's gesture in reaching out and gently passing her fingers through Sandro's hair is one the unwary might read as one of "renewal," of "life"; she, the fount. But the spring is dry; the ground, hard.

Anna sought annihilation (though Antonioni in a timorous post mortem speculated that such was not the case) in a her-ringbone number of dashingly good taste; Claudia seeks a shared pity in a funereal black sack of utter plainness. The adventure began well, but ends badly.

Yet, in memory, what lingers of *L'Avventura* is its auspicious inceptive venturing. Here we had the makings of a modern *Odyssey*, by Heraclitus.

It should be kept in mind that *L'Avventura* is but the first part of Antonioni's trilogy. He did not stop with this sentimental action. Intuitive genius that he is, he, in the concluding movement of his great trilogy which traces the passage from morning light (though it bore a shadow—Claudia having brought along Fitzgerald's *Tender Is the Night* as reading for her Mediterranean adventure) into night (*La Notte*, 1961), and beyond, finding a perfection of formal symmetry in the closing seven-minute Roman Canto of *Eclipse*, sloughed off his despondent alienation and manfully faced the void.

In an address which Antonioni gave at the Centro Sperimentale (March 16, 1961), while in the midst of conceiving and realizing his great trilogy, he remarked that "perhaps one day cinema will...achieve the heights of abstraction.... Something of this sort is already taking place."

With *Eclipse* and its final image, "light around a dark center," Antonioni realized masterfully what he had alluded to: "the heights—of abstraction."

# Metaphysic in the Marketplace: Orson Welles' "Touch of Evil"

*Touch of Evil* was produced in 1956, and released in 1958 to an uncomprehending press:

> ...effect rather than substance...
> Howard Thompson, *New York Times* (May 24)

> ...shadows without substance.
> John Cutts, *Films and Filming* (July)

> ...so banal...
> Jeremy Brown, *Films in Review* (April)

One review condescendingly gave it the back-handed compliment of granting it "camp" status:

> ...it is a good bad movie, which is more
> fun...than the mediocre or even adequate.
> Gerald Weales, *The Reporter* (June 26)

166

One voice, raised against the negative critical consensus, was Stanley Kauffmann in *The New Republic*

> If *Touch of Evil* had come from France...it would be playing...the art houses [rather than, as was the case, having been "dumped into neighborhood theatres in New York"], and phrases like "structural plasticity" and "delicate diabolism" would be filling the critical air.

Europe, that summer, was to validate Kauffmann's insight; the film was adjudged "best" at the Brussels World Fair.

Some seven years after its release in the middle of the decade which, with the advent of the "New Wave," came to be known as the age of the film generation, criticism had, to a degree caught up with the sophistication of creation, and the new-found genre of *"film noir"* was seen as the rubric under which *Touch of Evil* fell, Peter Cowie identifying it as "essentially a film of darkness."[1]

But "darkness" is not the dimension or extension of works having a metaphysical reach. Thus, even by its friendly critics, *Touch of Evil* appeared to be consigned, in English consideration at least, to the realm of the mundane.

Then, *mirabile!* (in Cowie) there appeared, from behind the Iron Curtain, an insight, couched though it may have been in a negative dismissal of the work, that sensed what Orson had been up to:

> This depressing...film...shows a morbid...shift of realistic concepts towards metaphysics...
>> Sergei Gerasimov

---

[1] Peter Cowie, *The Cinema of Orson Welles* (New York: Da Capo Press, 1983).

*Metaphysics*!—at last, if with scornful disdain, critical recognition of where Orson is at!

For *Touch of Evil* is *not* "a preposterous melodrama" (Cutts). It is a Nietzschean tragedy of the abyss set on the dark face of the moon. It is a metaphysical mystery, an alchemic rite of inversion. It looks into the abyss. And, as in *The Birth of Tragedy*, from deep within the dark comes light—the luminous Nietzschean afterimage.

As *the* philosopher averred:

> ...the basic metaphysic is the inversion
> of values: truth out of deception, a self-
> less act out of self-interest, things of
> highest value from this inferior world,
> this labyrinth of delusion...[2]

Orson Welles is an anomaly in American commercial cinema. His works, and his life, have been dedicated to the bringing of a philosophic vision to the screen. As he has written:

> I believe...my films...are...a search
> ...[in] a labyrinth...[3]

And, long before structuralism became a major branch of film study, he was practicing its principles. As he noted:

> What interests me in cinema is abstraction.[4]

Wellesian cinema is a conspectus of abstract vision: a whispering gallery of fatuous small talk that has the ring of truth, a

---

[2] Friedrich Nietzsche, *Beyond Good and Evil*, in *Basic Writings of Nietzsche*, ed. Walter Kaufmann (New York: Modern Library, 1968).

[3] Terry Comito, "Touch of Evil," *Film Comment* (Summer, 1971).

[4] Ibid.

corridor of mirrors leading to the still point at the center of life's revolving dumbshow, a baroque geometry of desire and, at one and the same time, a Vedic calculus of cancellation.

*Touch of Evil's* close pattern of reflected images in sight, sound, and action serves to effect a Nietzschean transmutation—of value. For Welles, at a deep subconscious level, is a nature philosopher. His art, in its essence, as in Empedocles' line of syzygies joining love-hate, does not treat action but, rather, the inexorable press of supramoral force that issues in brilliant cinematic tropes.

No film is richer in symbolic schemata:

—the metallic echo of the feedback on the walkie-talkie recorder;

—the grotesque inverted mirror image of the hero in the sump pond as he is about to wash his sullied hand;

—the life of duplicity: an upholder of the law on the surface, but, in reality, a deceitful framer of aliens unfortunate enough to be suspect in capital crimes;

—the repeated leaving of the incriminating cane at the scene of the crime;

—the ritualistic repetition of the compulsive act of murder by strangulation, we are led to believe, in a vain attempt to atone for his neglect of his young wife, his failure to protect her, or, as we may glean, his actually having murdered her (!), and his attempt to frame yet another young wife of a lawman—who also fails to protect her from base abuse;

—the repeated ritual of sacrifice, taking a bullet in his game leg to save his buddy, Pete, and taking a "second (fatal) shot" from Pete that binds them in death;

—the formal repetition of the motif of destruction: the burst of flame in the dynamiting of the car at the opening, and of the flash of waters taking the hero at the close;

—and, finally, the return of Hank to Tanya, to the woman, and *her* return to him, after his death, to speak his epitaph:

He was some kind of man...

From "this inferior world, this labyrinth of delusion"—to an "inversion of values": from the "evil" of self to the virtue of an all-forgiving, all-understanding humanity, to love. From the crescent scythe of age, the crone, to the "dark madonna" of Mexican folkways, to the womb of the new moon.

As Kane was reborn in the recovery of the dark sun under the volcano in the dreamed retrieval of youth and the fullness of a mother's love enwrapped in the secret emblem, "Rosebud," and in its inversionary annihilation in the fiery furnace transmuting ice to fire, and substance to insubstantial vapor, Hank, in a like ritual, was regenerate in the love of a dark (once "Blonde") Venus, and in the selfless *and* faulted love of his closest friend (Pete-Bernstein).

A film of darkness, as Cowie says?

Rather, a work of light, of mystic renewal beyond the dark eclipse of Being.

There is an ancient grandeur to the masterworks of Orson Welles.They are moving sacrifices on the altar of the black sun and the black moon.


*Images*:

Hands move, setting a timer.

The music pulses, setting up an intense inner pacing. Tension builds.

This opening image evidences the genius of Orson Welles as a *maitre de la mise en scène*; with utmost economy each element of the decor establishes the heavy air of menace that is to darken the total action: the cowl-like aluminum facing of the cheap kitchen timer catches the light in a blinding glare; the indicator casts a shark-fin shadow; and the bands of friction tape over the goggle-eyed battery trademarks give an S-M intimation of bondage and blindfold menace.

The furtive figure darts right, the camera following; the effect is very fluid, sinuous, unsettling in its sudden dark thrust.

Held in still frame, we can make out the identity of the darting figure; it is Manuelo Sanchez (Victor Millan), shabbily genteel in his Robert Hall three-button grey flannel suit, with each button tackily buttoned. He is running full out past the "Flamenco" galleria liquor store that flanks a Spanish-style round arched arcade.

Sanchez crosses right; his looming shadow ominously tails his dark flight across a wall of seedy posters:
—"Follies," girls-girls-girls shall garnish the scene and propel the action—the inceptive rape-murder of Hank Quinlan's wife thirty years ago (or his killing her for having adulterously betrayed him) that set him off on his lifelong quest for revenge; and, though only hinted in the action, Marcia Linnekar's manipulation of Sanchez in getting him to blow her daddy to kingdom come;
—"Mexico—Taxco," a name resonant with the ring of silver plunder from two long centuries of colonial exploitation; the theme of Yanqui appropriation of native black gold, while never made explicit, is implicitly present in every shot of that most depressing of depressed oil towns, Los Robles;
—"Atlas"—tires, no doubt, that tool over Los Robles' chuck holes, as the white-walls on Rudy Linnekar's Chrysler Imperial.
The verticals of the posters break up in the rapid follow-pan which tracks Sanchez's mission of destruction. The breakup of image is to find a concrete (if pulverizing) equivalent in the dynamite blast.
Nothing, repeat, nothing (!) in Welles is adventitious. All elements are precisely calculated aspects of the film's design.

Framed by a classic symmetry, black walls shouldering convergently toward a lowering dusk sky, Sanchez, a dark figure, crouches behind Linnekar's '56 Imperial convertible, its chromium armorial stripes and side mirror gleaming. Stealthily Sanchez moves away after planting the bomb beneath the car's trunk.

Craning back and up rapidly, with the feral motive of a night creature, a bat, which rises to pounce, Rudy and "Lisa" (Zita) enter the death car; a bullet-headed big shot and his blonde bimbo out for a night on the town are caught in the strong parking lot lighting, two cruciform figures that synchronously, with ritualistic precision, open the car's doors, so it too becomes a cross of light, and enter the engine of destruction.

The death car is to "cross" the border, heading North, there to encounter annihilation by fire. The invisible international boundary line that divides two cultures has a psychic equivalent in the festering we/they antagonism that poisons the air of Los Robles.

It is not stretching matters to discern in this image's extreme complexity of symbolic form a dimension one seldom encounters in American film—the metaphysical. The text may be based on a pulp policier by Whit Masterson[5] but the subtext, the ur text, is by John Donne.

Rising above the roofline, the roof assumes a dark dentate shape, a crocodile's snout, the fin of a shark, the shadow of a bat; moving behind this black mass, the death car is devoured by the minatory forms of night.

It is as though the film's opening were to be seen through the eyes of the Mexican sky god, Zotzilaha, the Bat God of volcanic fires and earthquakes. An earth-shaking volcano is about to erupt in the back of Rudy Linnekar's Imperial.

The night flight of the camera tracks its invisible quarry, Rudy Linnekar's Imperial, in its move sinister, obscured by the black bulk of the Flamenco "Liquor" mart, its garish vertical neon and giant black-lettered sign proclaiming the sale of an unfailing anodyne for the desperation of existence in the backwater hole, a beckoning beacon of annihilation to which Hank has often had cause to repair.

---

[5] Whit Masterson, *Badge of Evil* (New York: Dodd, Mead, 1956).

Welles once made cinema history, in *Kane*, with his famous model-shot descent through the skylight of the El Rancho roadhouse outside Atlantic City. This is no model of a floozie's universe on the skids; it's the real McCoy, on a scale of 1 : 1, Hank Quinlan's stamping ground for his boozy toots South of the border, a sleazy inclined plane heading straight down to Tanya's blue movies, with hot chili on the side.

Rudy pulls out of the alley and onto Los Robles' main drag, a poor man's Toledo lined by pseudo-moorish colonnades of neon arches and columns blazoned with garish girlie posters flaunting naughty keyhole poses.

Flaubert has written that genius is in details. On the basis of the infinite calculation revealed in this fleeting scene which sets the stage for the limping (Oedipal?) passage of our anti-hero, Orson Welles fully validates the accolade, "boy genius," pinned on him by the studio's flacks.

No director, repeat, *no* director, bar none, is his equal in design cunning, in command of the essence of cinema, *mise en scène*. He is the master, and this his masterpiece.

Tracking back, holding the Imperial center frame as in the cross-hairs of a gun sight, the camera picks up one of Los Robles' "finest," making the streets safer for the street walkers and their clientele, raising a white gloved hand for a vagrant crosstown car, staying momentarily the progress of Rudy and his heavy date on their collision course with a detonator cap and eight sticks of dynamite.

Pulling back further, the convertible moves off. A street vendor appears from out of nowhere and trundles his wagon across the deserted street like a baggy pants comic (say, Chico Marx with his "get your tootsie-fruitsie ice-a-cream" cart in *A Day at the Races*, 1937), guided by two arrows formed by white lane-markers which suggestively plot the coordinates of an irrational synchronicity of event—as the cart hits that arrow all hell will break loose off-frame! And, as though this were a Tom and Jerry cartoon, the mind races in a mad calculation—how far down that bowling alley of a street will the blast blow the Chico lookalike?

But the feared moment passes; he makes it across safely.

Continuing the pullback, frame center finds a new focus of interest—Janet Leigh, jacket jauntily swung across a broad shoulder. Out of the corner of one's eye one catches, in profile, a moustachioed Latino she has in tow—Charlton Heston? *why* couldn't it have been Harold Huber?—clad in a somber business suit that has all the marks of a Sears "Best-Buy" in its stodgy drape. The romantic duo, the stars for whom the studio gave the okay to the production, they being considered money-in-the-bank at the box office, attract attention. But, all but buried in mysterious shadow, another center of interest deserves notice: a bench presents a symbolic decalcomania to the startled eye—two disembodied hands thrust up between a commerical medallion in a gesture of terror, fingers splayed, as in horror at the soon to be unleashed lethal fury.

The kiss, the clinch, a hallowed Hollywood convention, though coming here at the beginning, and not, as is usually the case, at the end. The pose is stiff; it is apparent Charlton (Mike "Miguel" Vargas, Mexico's ace narc officer) can't unbend, even on this, his honeymoon.

But the problematic presence of romance-romance in a hardnosed police drama aside, this setup gets us down to cases: Orson makes the climactic actional payoff worthy of his brilliant three-minute one-take prologue. Most directors would choose to focus on *the* action—slo-mo bodies in the air, but Welles approaches this key action abstractly; he chooses to treat it formally, with classic restraint. We do not see the explosion. We hear it, off-camera, and witness its destructive onslaught indirectly as a blinding flash that makes the image of the lovers bloom with the actinic overload. Graphically, it is a moment of suprematist order in the expressionist maelstrom, the frame a field of cyclopean architectonic forms—the white of a stucco wall blazoned with a radiant corona, an arrow wedge of reflective coping catching the full incandescence of the dynamite flash.

We cut, in the first cut in the film, to the death car at the fatal instant of fiery destruction.

A mask of death, an Aztec icon—eyes of obsidian, a crest of flaming plumage. In a further marvel of evanescent form, a rapacious beak of flame engulfs the death car. (See Figure 4.)

The firebird pounces!

No phoenix this—a daemonic burst pounds the earth and shatters, leaving nothing.

Another bird of prey—molting slightly, and grounded by a game leg—a wily old owl: Captain Hank Quinlan (Orson Welles). (See Figure 5.)

His beatup heap, a bunty '49 two-door Ford that crusty old Henry—never one-of-the-boys "Hank," he—must have had a hand in designing, such a tadpole holdover in a new sea of riggish tailfins, bounces to a shot-shocks stop; the door swings open and a gargantuan pot belly heaves into view. A massive grunt and creak as the car seat springs give under the overload and Hank makes his *big* entrance. And Hank (Orson) *is* large: big Q can't be framed by anything manmade—a car, or a pesky law code. Hank's as big as the horizon. And it's not just a case of this take-charge guy having a swelled head. It has to do with tragic scale—Orson didn't play Lear in the Big Apple, to houses of frumpy hausfraus bussed in from New Rochelle, for nothing. On the street where Willie Loman lugged his sample cases around for a record run, Welles, the tragic thespian, felt

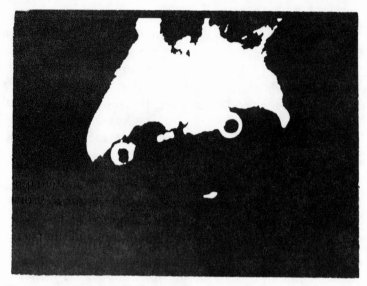

*Figure 4.*   Mask of death, an Aztec icon—

*Figure 5.*   Another bird of prey...Captain Hank Quinlan (Orson
             Welles).

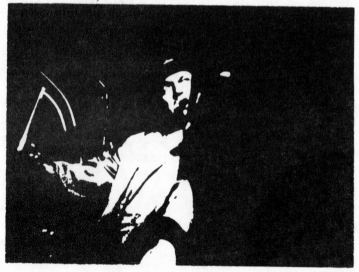

driven to be "bound upon a wheel of fire," to essay the grandest of tragic roles, a towering alazon figure brought low, in the classic tragic action, by a fatal flaw and by fate. While Hank might not cotton to the use of such twenty-five-cent terms and would scoff at the notion he was some kind of demigod (and Orson in his putty nose would join in the scornful mock—if "Rosebud" was "dollar-book Freud" to him, Quinlan-as-archetype would strike him as phoney as a plug nickel) Hank and Lear are in the same big league.

André Bazin found Hank "monumental, enormous... olympian...monstrous."[6]

And Welles, he is more than an actor; his is an electric presence, like heat lightning as a storm approaches. When Welles takes the stage on this entrance, the screen lifts to a new dimension—the archetypal.

"Hank and the Boys—or—you can always judge a man by the tilt of his Adams hat." There's a circle of energy in the way a brim frames a face, sets it off, or just lets it lie there.

The latter extreme is evident in Chief Gould (Harry Shannon), a rock-jawed John Law. His fedora has a knife brim with sharp crease; maybe he's seen too many Dick Tracy B-movies and has taken a fashion tip from the natty crime stopper. Frame left, in the full light of "Rudy Linnekar's bonfire," the Chief plays downstage, semi-profile.

But, frame right—there *he* is! Hank Quinlan! Gould doesn't stand a prayer of even being noticed with Hank in the picture.

And there's a matter of hat brims, as well as bulk, working in Hank's favor. There's a certain air of rumpled vulnerability to that boyish cocking of his brim; not exactly upturned, but a soft roll that sits loosely high on his brow—this guy may be no easy mark, but he's open. A regular Joe—you can't help liking Hank.

---

[6] André Bazin, *Orson Welles, a Critical View*, tr. Jonathan Rosenbaum (New York: Harper & Row, 1978).

But those eyes—they *do* look a mite beady. And those lips, now that we're giving him the once over, they do seem to have a twisted look that much as says, "Come off it, Buster." Yet again, it's not easy to get Hank tagged dead to rights: there's a funny smile buried somewhere in those puffy suitcases he's carrying beneath his eyes. Complex—that's the word for Hank.

And, in the background, never one to make himself noticed when the head man, Hank, is making his presence felt, is hat brim #3—the light hat of a good-guy, yet complex too in its rakish tilt that matches the rakish smirk caught in strong crosslight. It's Hank's sidekick, Pete (Joseph Calleia)—always slightly more than slightly gauche; you'd tab him anywhere as a local yokel.

Welles, who has a positive genius for casting character roles (it takes one to know one), shone in casting Calleia, the perfect Sancho to his Don. That self-satisfied smirk he always pulls as Hank gets off a good one is one of the minor joys of this backwater saga.

Pete's in his element, for sure, basking in the glow of Hank's take-charge swaggering, but, such is the complexity of Welles' vision, framing this midcentury epigone of the Keystone Kops there is a presentiment of a dark cast: frame left, silhouetted against the blazing aftermath of the dynamite blast, is a leather-jacketed officer of the law, and, frame right, the shadowy profile of Assistant D.A. Al Schwartz (Mort Mills), eventually to be Pete's (and Hank's) nemesis.

The severity of Schwartz's horn rims and the determined set of his jaw, the humorlessness of his expression, are in striking contrast to Pete's amiable schlepping. Pete and Schwartz: the masks of Folly, and of a stern Justice; in a frame, an emblematic rendering of the moral schema underlying the larger action.

Leaving the scene of a carnage for one of carnal pleasure—
we have the return after many moons of a moony Hank
Quinlan to Tanya's (Marlene Dietrich's) place, candy bar at
the ready.

Only Welles could have visualized this scene, almost solar-
ized, so great is the contrast of light and dark, his face a
half-moon, flabby jowls all too apparent in the cruel crosslight:
"You should lay off those candy bars.... You're a mess, honey."
And the wonder of the Wellesian eye: the scimitar curve of the
moorish portico framing Hank's massive form, a lunar crescent in the curving beam, symbol of the lunar crone, of Saturn,
age, an age that has taken its toll; once hootch and hot chili,
Hank's weakness now is Oh Henrys and Baby Ruths. The
scythe has cut. Hank is now less than a man: Silenus, Pappus, a
subject of risible scorn from the birth of the comic spirit, and a
source of bitter loss.

Close-up, Dietrich, a quarter of a century after *Blonde
Venus* (1932), a dark Venus, yet, still, the constancy of the
exotic mask, the hungry hollows beneath high cheekbones, the
lustful flaring of nostrils, the brows' disdainful arch, jaded eyes
that cast shadows as they catch the light—still the voluptuary
mask Josef von Sternberg enshrined in the annals of erotic
cinema.

Spangled, beaded—a high Aztec lunar goddess, demanding
sacrifice on her altar at the crest of the fire pyramid; the dream
goddess—Dietrich.

After thirty years on the force, Hank's so far over-the-hill he
can't even see the hill anymore. It's back to the smelly turkey
ranch for him, for you-can't-go-home-again, or make a go of it
at a house of joy again. Oh, one can drop in on Tanya, for it is
not strange "desire should so many years outlive performance"
(*Henry IV*, II). You can stand there in the middle of her parlor

amid the dusty pendant lampshades with their voile fluting and crimped rosettes and fringe and the lace curtains on their sagging rods and feel the room sag as Tanya's eyes tell you "No dice."

Shades of *Shanghai Express* (1932): the veil of smoke, etching an icon of Eve; or are we on a Tijuana local? And what matter it where, when this veil cannabic(?) caresses that incredible mask, those eyes with their delirious invitation to nirvanic rapture?

And the goddess's costume speaks of more than voluptuous release: motifs, of Aztec inspiration, in embroidered epaulettes and patches, in courses, diamond and chequered, bespeak the elemental conflict of sky and earth, of light and dark. And, above the ever-youthful bosom, beaded and pendant necklaces, jet and clear; clear above the right breast, jet above the heart. How subtly Orson (and his costume designer and art directors, Alexander Golitzen and Robert Clatworthy) devised the setting for this striking cameo—that is more than a mere cameo, that is the very center of the work's symbolic structure, a center that transforms a seamy *noir* into that cinematic rarity, a transcendent mystery.

In the bedizened alternation of white and black in the diamond, chequered, and circular motifs that frame the symmetry that is Dietrich is traced the metaphysical schema of fire and earth, of the wheeling sky in the calendric order of the Great Year, of sacrifice and renewal, that so lifts Tanya's penultimate line at the film's close to a meta-tragic reach. In Tanya (Dietrich) is to be found the pattern in Aztec codices and in the courses girting the fire pyramids of this highest of ancient cultures. Cortez and his conquistadors thought they had eradicated this Nietzschean-Artaudian theater of madness and cruelty (or so they deemed it in their awful ignorance of transcendent energies). Welles, in his B-budget masterpiece, relumed the pre-Columbian fire.

We find Susie, on the street—in the literal sense, though with such a nebbish for a hubby no one could blame her for being there in a figurative sense, on the make for a *Belle de Jour* dalliance. But intrigue, not sex intrigue, is the order of the day as she finds herself on the receiving end of a message from greasy Uncle Joe Grandi (Akim Tamiroff), the local vice lord who constitutes the prime target of that paragon of virtue, her husband, in name, if not in deed, Inspector Vargas.

The wheels (not wheels-within-wheels, just wheels) of Uncle Joe's (and Hank's—in a lapsed whiskey-sodden moment) fiendish, and oh so sappy, plot are rolling; the canary is about to step in the quicklime; Susie is Motel Mirador bound!

Make that Mirador Motel; no classy inversion for the likes of this fleatrap. (See Figure 6.)

The setting—in the middle of nowhere; minimal photorealism of anywhere on the shadow side of the moon or who-cares-where USA; sagebrush stubble, an alkali ribbon of dust waiting for the Santa Ana to do a fade to white on this view of the void. Unlisted by the AAA, and uninspected by the county health commissioner—Uncle Joe Grandi's Mirador Motel.

Architecturally *naif* and *primitif,* Venturi ugly, or "early nothing" (as Gloria Graham tabbed her seedy hotel room in Fritz Lang's *The Big Heat* (1953)): tacky aluminum window units and breezeway posts, as design accents to the boredom of concrete block construction, not to forget the vertically lettered sign (Venturi would nod approvingly) on a fluted column stuck out in a bare field—late (too late) deco. But no deco delite can lift the oppressive pall that hangs over this cellblock nightmare; ten units w. h.c. wtr., ten private little hells for the tired salesmen to flop in. The emptiness of the West in a decline that Spengler never dreamed of; the intra-terrestrial entropy of lives without purpose winding down in a sandwich of Clorox impregnated sheets over a rubber mattress cover.

Yet this nothing scene contains an aesthetic paradox: there

*Figure 6.*   The setting—in the middle of nowhere—Uncle Joe
Grandi's Mirador Motel.

*Figure 7.*   Susie raises the shade, as the sun sinks in the west and the
curtain rises on—Shock Teatro.

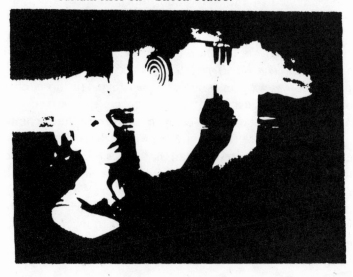

is an exhilarating lift in this postcard of the void, a secret energy in its wide-angled view of the roadside America vacua Bruce Davidson celebrates in his photodocumentations of the backroads of our memory and the interstate roadside rests for our kidneys. Hollywood never got out where we live (if you call that living). Here, for once, Orson Welles brought us a rare and privileged gift. Like a slightly demented Ralph Edwards, he dumped on us this wash of the blahs we've all seen receding in our rear view mirrors anywhere west of the Mississippi, as if to say, "This Is Your Life!" And it is—every gawdawful dull bit of it.

*Touch of Evil* is a movie; it has something to do with people on the move or on the skids (same difference), but that's not where it's at. *This* is where it's at—nowheresville.

And while forbidden delights await within, here we cannot tarry (for this is Welles, not Warhol); and Los Robles waits, anything but "lovely," if "dark and deep," and Orson has: "miles to go before" Susie beds down in her satin leotards and tries to get some beauty sleep.

> "Put out the light, and then put out the light."
> (*Othello* V ii)

Susie (Susan—a name that derives from the lotus, the sacred Egyptian soporific-hallucinogen; Welles did not idly choose to make the source novel's "Connie" "Susan," as in Susan Alexander Kane, she of the forget-me-not "Rosebud" paperweight), Susie, charmingly unaware of what's in her name or what's in store, beds down, well—inclines up, rather, provocatively propped on a pillow, awaiting the sweet hymeneal dreams of this her second unconsummated wedding night (while, meanwhile, back at the Rancho Grandi the benedict, "my darling Miguel," is hard at work on the case—duty calls (the idiot)); all that floral lace going to waste, zippers waiting to be unzipped, lips to be parted in a kiss.

But, hark, rescue of the drowsy maid is headed her way—

"So discord oft in music makes the sweet lay."
(*The Faerie Queene*, II ii)

"Pancho" (Valentin De Vargas) pipes some hot wax into
Susie's room on the Mirador Motel's Lafayette Radio mail-
order supersonic wall speaker, an aluminized monstrosity, a
concentric abomination. And the framing of this raucous eye-
sore is remarkable (is *anything* in Orson's decor not remarkable?): the surreal shadows of a minatory window frame form
an eye; the concentric iris of the speaker, an eye with a corneal
sty in the ring of a tacky roller-blind sash cord. And the eye has
a face: beneath the cyclopean eye, yawning wide, is a dentate
orifice. The effect is unsettling, this Wellesian twist on Lewis
Carroll: Susie-in-Sleazyland' or, taking another tack, Orson
tears a page from the book of Barthes and captures, as he so
admirably had in the utterly banal establishing shot of the
Mirador, *le degré zéro* of *le cinéma*. That "speaker," on second
look, looks like, and functions as, a drain. With the scrofulous
punks and dykes about to debouch their dismal debauch onto
Susie, the figure fits.

The nightman (Dennis Weaver),

Susie's harrying, as in a Jacobean tragedy, brings on a
prancing lunatic to do his mad dance—a scarecrow grin and
sudden turn, a skittish chicken swoop—making a mockery of
the victim's humiliation. A vertiginous disorientation is the
intent—and in the moonscape silence descried by Susie
through her window pane, it serves its dizzying purpose.

A phantasmagoria, passing strange, dizzying in its other-
worldly stillness—a sleeping crocodile mountain range and
two skies; stratus above, striate stratus; below, salt lick slivers

afire with the phosphorescent glow of the fading light from the falling sky caught in the stagnant waters.

And, stranger still, a spindly stanchion holding up the breezeway's overhang, three echt tubular steel rods that strike eerie Mephisto chords in this lunar prelude to the impending diablérie.

Susie, raising the shade, peeks out her window as the sun sinks slowly in the west and the curtain rises on—Shock Teatro. (See Figure 7.)

Graphic surrealism came to the screen in the Forties with the painterly kitsch of Dali's dream sequences. In this decade of Freudian discovery in Hollywood, Welles had also achieved the cinematic surrealism of the Fun House labyrinth and mirror maze in *The Lady from Shanghai* (1948). Here, the master of design has fashioned such a derangement of the senses as Beaudelaire would approve. And the formal beauty of the graphic handling—it is of such perfection one would wish to hold this image, to fix it in memory. It is a classic.

Consider the spiritual dimension of the figure: the whiteness, the purity of Leigh's brow, the precision with which it is cleft by the low desert horizon; there is about it an ethereality that raises the image above the earthbound to the empyrean. She is woman, in her two extreme guises of virgin and whore, an alabaster innocent and creature of the dark. Her hand, drawing out the cord of the venetian blind, is black as pitch, in contrast to the radiant brow. And the face bears the self-same duplicity: dexter, refulgently bathed in a streaming light; sinister, the dark crescent of the moon, her classic profile incised by shadow of blackest jet. The line of the cord is plotted with utmost care; in the subtle perfection of its geometry it intersects the central rod of the reflected stanchion's triadic form, echoing the three concentric rings about the center of the wall speaker. Three is the number of the visible phases of the moon. There is a fourth, the dark.

The malific aspect of nature is about to descend. And it is here prefigured.

The pockmarked door swings slowly open—and a less-than-spectral phantom invades the princess's less-than-castle keep. The bed chamber of a princess does not have plywood doors bruised by the pounding of loutish drunks or gypsum wallboard that suffers a similar defacement. And Prince Charming enters, not a simpering creep with a greasy Elvis pompadour.

But we are no longer in the age of chivalry, of knights errant on silver chargers; this is the age of venality, of leather and chain dullards astride their Harleys and Indians reeking of Castroil and Brylcreem.

Evil approaches, an obliterative shadow.

The startled faun and the cloven fiend, as dark flames rage on the satin pillow strewn with golden tresses.

And the dramatic calculation behind the set-up is sound: evil hinted at is more terrible in its suggested defilement than blatant depiction; yet that is what follows—a campy gang debauch of Miss Prim from Philadelphia. It could be held that this venture into Sam Fuller's earthy combat zone was far afield for Orson; trashy thrills are not amenable to abstract crystallographic analysis.

And, though we are to be told that Susie came out okay, in fact, neat as a pin and none the worse for wear from the sink of iniquity, one can be forgiven for taking it with a grain of saltpetre; Vargas, for all his superhero shadows and super-sleuth bugs, is still a schlemiel, a stock comic joke—a cuckold. Hank has his turkey ranch; Vargas is one (a cold turkey).

We find Hank in his cups, puffy-eyed, slack jawed, the heat of alcohol seeping through his sweaty pores, with a life saver "Cervesa" tequila logo tacked on the door behind him, though he's sinking fast and even Pete can't save him. All Pete can do, as he's been doing all their years together, is to be a good listener to Hank's sozzled tale of woe.

"Cervesa": cervix—of the neck?

Hank has just finished his dog-eared testimonial to the "clean and silent...the smart way to kill," as Pete hands him down his walking cane. The action attracts attention away from the dialogue. Hank has been maundering away under the influence. But wait! Listen again to what Hank was saying (under the distracting action of Pete's settling the bill with the bartender); Orson wrote the lines—they're not in the source novel. They supposedly give the motive for Hank's life of revenge. Examining them closely, suddenly Ron Gottesman's paper given at a Northwestern University Film Association Conference, "Who Really Killed Mrs. Quinlan?" snaps into focus. The answer: Hank Quinlan! It takes no gimlet-eyed cop to sense a shiftiness in the way Hank tells his story of how Mrs. Q. came to an untimely end, but Hank (Orson) breathes such authority into the telling it had us fooled, as it's fooled Pete all these years.

> HANK: Did I ever tell you the smart way to kill, Pete?...
> ...binding cord—
> (Very lowly) You don't leave fingerprints on a piece of string.

Question: would Hank, with his contempt for "the Mex," credit such a lowlife, who'd been getting his wife to two-time him, with being "right damn smart"? No, that's what Hank felt about numero uno.

And why, one might further ask, would the lover seek out his doxy at the packing plant when he was (for some ungodly reason that makes no sense at all) out to do her in?—when he had the lady alone, vulnerably alone, at their love nest? Rather, wouldn't the packing plant be the likely place a jealous husband would confront an errant wife?

And from his MO in framing Latinos ever since, why are we to assume that Hank as a rookie cop was pure as the driven snow and not the slippery customer he's been these past forty years?

And the charge is supposed to stick—on this flimsy flapdoodle of mere opinion, from a most unreliable source: "We all knew it—" indeed.

Hank had been a mite too clever, or not clever enough: he's strangled his two-timing missus with a cord, leaving no incriminating murder instrument wherewith to frame the "halfbreed" who'd "taken" his manhood.

And Tanya knew all this. When he began to hit the bottle hard, she'd have put two and two together.

And over his body she could come to say: "He was some kind of man."

The last word, "man," gains heavy weight read in this light; he had been un-manned; but, and here's the tricky part, Eros and Thanatos are very close—his love for his buddy, Pete, went deeper than the sexual: he took Pete with him (as Pete wished to go) as an act of all-too-frail humanity, as a "perverse" act of "love."

For the S-M impulse is deeply engrained; it is present in tragedy where violence is the essential overt action, and in all rites of sacrifice—as in the "cruel" Aztec fire rite.

Tanya "knows," in the depth of her being, what "man" is capable of—of murder, of others and of oneself. And she accepts this stern dictate.

*Touch of Evil* is a most subtle engine of (psychic) destruction (*and* construction); we have proof in this seemingly throwaway drunk scene. How easily it is overlooked, this hidden flaw in Hank—his *total* duplicity. But, with it in mind, his subsequent pogrom against the swart despoiler(s) is understandable; and even more deplorable. For the Aztec sacrifice was to renew the sun, and not (vainly) to erase a stain on one's manhood.

A metal door slams—its explosion reverberating in the hollow reaches of the Hall of Records. Pete, entering, sets off a detonation that reflects back to the previous scene—the "gang bang"—or so one might surmise from the "Hold her legs!" admonition of one of the leather fetishists as we left Susie, beleaguered.

And reflects further back still, to the delayed-reaction time bomb Hank set when he planted the dynamite in Sanchez's shoebox, that is about to go off—on Pete. For he's about to learn the jig is up on Hank's capers, with him as accessory.

Heading into the home stretch, Orson and Marlene. What a team they made!

In all seriousness, "Hank and Tanya"—there was, in this pairing, the makings of the earthy charm of Glenda Farrell and Barton MacLane in the "Torchy Blane" Bs of the late Thirties, of the hard-boiled lovers—Paul Douglas and Linda Darnell, Gable and Harlow, Bogey and Baby. Orson's waddling around Tanya's while she bounced insult humor off him made up one third of the charm of *Touch of Evil*. The other two thirds are the "love affairs" between Hank and Pete and between Orson's (and cinematographer Russell Metty's) camera and Los Robles, that seemingly endless series of discoveries, as in Elliott Erwitt's wry photodocumentations, of the empty jokes time makes of our little efforts to leave the world a little better for our having stumbled around in it; a love affair with two climaxes of kitsch good/bad taste: Uncle Joe's Mirador Motel, ca. 1948, and Tanya's place, ca. 1918.

And here we are again—Hank has come back "home" to Tanya's, but Thomas Wolfe had it tabbed and Tanya won't take him in, giving him the brush: "...go home." To what? his turkey ranch?

But, viewed on a higher plane, in the cold symmetry of Hank's last encounter with woman there is a metaphysical

dimension: the scene is at once exotic and mundane. Tanya—
ring-encrusted hands, rain-forest wallpaper, an Indian motif
jacket to protect from the chill of the night; and then the
revelatory detail: in the crowded folds of the drapery, a circular
geometric quadrifoil ringed by eight chevrons. The figure is
compass like, and calendric; it constitutes a stylized rendering
of the Aztec calendar stone which plotted the Great Year at
fifty-two year intervals, the eternal round when the skies
returned to the cyclic point of renewal.

The calendar wheel turns, for the sky and for woman
(Tanya). She is in touch with the spiritual powers of fate; on a
table nearby there is a Tarot deck. There is a tragic distance in
her gaze. She sees what is to come. She sees beyond Hank to
the emptiness into which he is about to fall. His future is "all
used up."

And, at the close, her voice is to see further still—
transcendentally, into the past which vindicates, despite the
press of moral sanction.

*Touch of Evil* is a remarkable film, indeed; in an action that,
on the surface, is a mere dark melodrama, a *noir*, there is a
metaphysical reach. This image of Tanya and its resonance of
the searing vision of an ancient native culture most subtly limns
the exceptional turn at the close.

The beehive photoelectric cells of Vargas' tape-recorder
receiver unit, sixty-six eyes gathering the darkness of Hank's
past, sixty-six little whorls of glass, a multiform "Rosebud"
paperweight, with, as reflected snow scenes, the mask-like eyes
of Vargas's white shirt, preserving in iron oxide a past that
Hank would forget, but cannot. The beads of condensed mois-
ture on the granitic metal casing, catching the light, create a
glistening night sky, with the ovoid aperture of the electric cells
forming a black hole in the firmament into which pours the
impulsion to the nihilistic void. For though, as the tragic hero

must, he struggles against stern necessity to the last, he is beaten, and knows it. There is no high tragic afflatus to this final descent, but a coalescence of the convergent forces of doom, a massive weight pressing down inexorably as the gravity that quells all vital matter; this, the law in tragedy, and in physics.

But there is another level to existence—the metaphysical. This is the level at which Welles's two great films function: in *Kane*'s fiery furnace a rite of transformation effects a liberating transmutation of gross matter; the weight of care is mystically lifted. And in *Touch of Evil* a similar transcendence is symbolically present: a mystic release is to be effected by the elegiac energies that counter the entropic drift.

The touch—of agape.

Fatally wounded, Pete reaches out to stay his fall, clutching the hand which delivered the fatal dart. And the hand so often clasped in a bond of friendship which the world could not sever, now, in a sudden parting, leaves the mark of mortality on the hand that exacted cruel vengeance on hands clamped by lethal electrodes, hands which in their spasms of death never reached out in their fall to touch their killer.

And killer he truly is. The awful selfishness of his life is revealed in his look as his last victim falls; he is not looking at his victim—he looks at his hand, at its sullied state. His is the role of villainous villain of Tourneur's tragedies of blood. Such a protagonist is unknown in the mindlessness of Hollywood; he is an anachronistic presence on a double feature screen; his proper home is Blackfriars; his audience, the metaphysical wits of the Jacobean court. Welles is a wonder for having so much as broached this stern subject. But the dark vein is only touched; the point is not driven home. Had the action consistently pursued this harsh line of unregenerate egoism it would have had the evil fascination of Iago.

But in this, his masterwork as an actor, Welles, with his long career in classic theater as guide, chose to temper the severe dismissal this image elicits. In this he took his cue from another peerless Shakespearean model—"fat Jack" (Henry IV, II).

But the Bard, writing a history play, was ruled by politick and banished his lovable ruffian. And Orson was, in a deeply touching sense, writing a "character," that literary form of satiric biographical sketch popular at court, with the subject— himself. Yet a satiric dismissal was not his purpose. He had read Coleridge (in *Kane*, the Xanadu aspect was his idea, not Mankiewicz's). And, as he composed Tanya's closing epitaph to Hank Quinlan (and to himself in this part he did not so much play as live), he might well have had Coleridge's epitaph to himself in mind:

> That he, who...with toil of breath,
> Found death in life, may here find life in death.

To S.T., the discovery was to be through prayer.

To Orson, the way was mystic.

He has written that he would not take a role in a film that he did not feel dominated the action. In *Touch of Evil*, as in *Kane* (call it megalomania; call it mystery) he would, though it blinks the whole moral order, impose his will on the void. Hubris? Yes, in the tradition of Sophocles, Shakespeare, Nietzsche, Artaud.

Stark contrast, a mask carved by one cruel cross-light, an arch of shadow staring, disbelieving, falling ravaged.

Forget the plot, the creaking mechanism that led to, and follows, this spasm. Register it—let it burn in. We are privi- leged to witness the aching desideratum of *Lear*—the death of Lear's Fool.

*Touch of Evil?*—the touch of mortality, a most affecting *memento mori*, the agon beyond the heath, in close-up. (See Figure 8.)

*Figure 8.* *Touch of Evil?*—the touch of mortality, a most affecting *memento mori,* the agon beyond the heath, in close-up.

*Figure 9.* Quinlan, a monumental mass—basilisk eyes staring in the final declension into death.

Expressionist zone lighting and a massing of form and thrust in the field sinister; the vast bulk of Quinlan, the putty face with a soiled felt corona, and the jagged lines of lapel and knifing glare of the loosened tie's rayon lining, the blood-stained hand, dreadful in its pendulous flaccidity: Hank has found his level—a monster of the deep.

The undulant reflection of the protagonist as the end approaches; unlike that earlier "monster," that "Octopus of the Press," Charles Foster Kane, this iconic image is not of a mystic tranquillity discovered in the infinitude of a corridor of mirrors, the past recaptured, clasped, in the Coleridgean "wondrous world of glass"; here, the hand is open, the digits splayed in crests of fire and shadow, open to the awful emptiness they have wrought. No distant echo of Coleridgean transcendence sounds in this infernal vision. The livid refulgence of that lunar visage, the incandescent flash-point of a lifelong burning glass of self-contempt, thunders with the annihilative revulsion of Othello: (V ii):

> Roast me in sulphur.
> Wash me in steep-down gulfs of liquid fire.

Alternatively, considered in light of the subsequent high-angle geometrizing of despair, the image could be read as an ironic parody of the magic crystallomantic mirror of Pythagoras, in which the reflection of the moon divined the future. For there is no future—"it's all used up."

Kane had his Xanadu, his warehouse of yesterdays.

The Boschian high aspect recalls the final crane shot above the heaped treasures and "junk," with a striking symbolic difference: this is no moving take leading to the fiery furnace; here, in a set shot, the angle is straight down into the consuming fire. There is a strange radiance in the turbid waters, a

Yeatsian enantiodromia, an inversionary shocking of opposites, of empyrean and Phlegethon; and, stranger still, the objects
strewing the scene have astrological provenance—constellations
of Aquarius (the Water Bearer—the washtub) and Gemini (the
Twins—the two open chambers of an abandoned suitcase), the
two zodiacal signs of duality, of inversionary dissolution and
the immanence of release; and, as well, an astrological "trine"
(the deltoid cluster of litter), though the convergence of malefic
circumstance would appear to make a bitter mockery of the
evolutionary-constructive principle—until one remembers
Tanya's gesture of grace in the offing.

Surely a symbolic laving of the frame, and yet this does not
exhaust Welles's amazingly fertile powers of symbolic creation: by the waters' edge, on a soiled cushion, as much in the
discard as old Hank, a black pregnant shape appears—the
shape reads (again) two ways: as a dragon dexter, and as a
salamander sinister. It suggests a shadow form, these two
fabulous mythological creatures, to the light of Hank's crouch-
ing toad. Amazing—this conspectus of mythic energies: in the
salamander, the spirit of transmutational fire; in the dragon,
the gnostic symbol of fiery dissolution; in the toad, the infernal
aridity that devours. The galactic flare of the sump pond shall,
as death approaches, consummate this combust imagery,
bathing the body in a fiery glory.

The ostensible action, Pete shoots Hank.

In the race of the action this is what impresses the eye. But,
held in memory, what a formal and symbolic order emerges!

Consider the way the human component conjoins the
opposed energies of cone and circle; the way the lethal object
casts a long shadow, as though it had a dual target. As indeed,
it does; in killing Hank, Pete figuratively kills himself. The
boys are a team; what could Pete be without Hank? Stan
without Ollie? Break up the act and the show closes.

Then note the symbolic (and formal) order of the decor. For

this, the climactic thrust that takes the protagonist, the quartering of the frame, with the corner of the balustrade projecting precisely into the frame so as to fill the lower right quarter, is a striking instance of the intricacy of Wellesian design. The quartering of space bears a resonance of the Donnean (and Aztec) metaphysical compass; it is as though the gun barrel were the celestial-infernal axis, and the shot, down at Hank below the Roman style bridge, were to have issued in stern judgment from above.

Further evidence of the complexity of Welles' symbolic design is to be discovered in the decorative masonry garland flanking the fallen warrior, Pete. It is fashioned with utmost cunning, being a stylized rendering of a sunflower, with decorative button as root, emblematic in Roman myth of the emergence of light from the darkness, of Mithras from the cave.

Why should this motif of the triumph of light over darkness occur at this darkest of moments in the film's action?

That Orson intended this moment and action, the act of the slaying of one's other self (so close is the affinity between Hank and Pete), to have a mystic dimension is clear from an anecdote concerning the production. Welles suggested "that the gunshot which kills [Hank]...be eliminated from the sound track," though the editor, Aaron Stell, "could not understand why, and Welles finally left the gunshot in."[7]

The sad creative limits facing the director—unable to convince his closest confederate, the editor who cuts his images, to catch his pulse of feeling—aside, the fact that Orson intended this key moment to be removed from reality bears stressing.

Perhaps Orson, like Hank, was following where his intuition led, playing a hunch he felt in his bones.

Or perhaps he was following the deep archetypal thread into the Jungian unconscious. As he stated:

---

[7] Charles Higham, *The Films of Orson Welles* (Berkeley: University of California Press, 1971).

> I believe my films...are...a search
> [in] a labyrinth,...[and] the
> searcher wants to lose himself...

To fall into a sea of flames—to lose one's self: in this there is a concise definition of the dark aspect of Wellesian gnosis—as in the myth of the minotaur, descent into the fiery maze, into the cave of the beast, and transcendent emergence in a violent rite.

Pete slumps to the ground in death; his hat, dislodged, falls slowly out of the frame, a falling object in a world in decline, a lunar disc in a descending arc.

For one must fall—to rise; as Hank, fatally wounded, is about to fall—to "rise" in a liquid burst of fire.

Hank, life draining and close to death (as in *Kane*) transformed by the solemn rite of passage; (as in *Kane*) sovereign in majesty, a monumental mass, head hunched down on the massive torso as, pierced in its vital center by the lethal bullet, gravity exerts its inexorable press on the vast bulk; the unearthly glow on the crown; the undulant shadow cast by the brim on the crepuscular countenance; and from deep within the sombre shade, basilisk eyes, heavy-lidded, staring with a languid topor in the final declension into death. (See Figure 9.)

The yawning blackness of the pit beckons, and yet across this void passes a gentle gesture: soundlessly, the dove-like fleck of Pete's fedora softly brushes the friend he loved, touching him in death, as they had touched in life.

*Touch of Evil?* The film was misnamed by its producing studio. The film, in all its darkness, is a manifest of the touch of love. Love, not suspense, is its impetus. Though critically classified as a *film noir*, it goes beyond the irony of *noir* to a singular complex of dramatic modes found signally in late Elizabethan and Jacobean tragedy. It is a dark romance, and a transcendent tragedy—the alchemic joining of the two metallic dragons—the fixity of sulphur, and the volatility of quick-silver—in a transmutation of the dross of existence into a quintessential bond of perfect trust, a consummation that failed, that ends in separation, for this is a *dark* romance. But—and this is the wonder of *Touch*—love transcends any flaw of character, as Hank's dying words and Tanya's epitaph are so movingly to demonstrate.

Jean Renoir has stated that a director (*auteur*) makes but one film in his career, over and over.

This image of the moment of death, the first extreme close-up, and in a sudden false-reverse (the only one), has a strangely familiar thematic and dramatic ring: *Kane* also has a false-reverse at Kane's pharaoh-like progress with the "Rosebud" paperweight in hand across the corridor of mirrors, this momentary disorientation of screen direction pointing the shift to the plane of remembrance in extreme close-up, aged lips uttering the sacred mantra, as Hank, with his last breath, in a line heavy with irony, recalls the distant past when the blood bond was forged: "Pete—that's the second bullet I stopped for you."

Hank's last thought is of the friend who blindly followed him in his descent, faithful to a point, Yet, with the approach of death, as beads of sweat appear on the grizzled face, there is no trace of bitterness in Hank's expression. Love encompassing, rather; cancelling all. Neither is there the slightest hint of remorse; only the gleam of fond recall. The tragic hero does not bend as the concentric forces of fate (and character) close upon him. Nor does he break. He stands—until the fatal fall.

Straight down, the fall and the angle of view; the body a white standing figure, quickly receding until the sudden engulfment in a fury of waters. (See Figure 10.)

Shining above, the coruscating reflections of two car head-lights dazzle the dark. The triad of light has the enhanced clarity of a photograph from outer space, as of the image

*Figure 10.* The fatal fall—straight down, the body a white standing figure, until the sudden engulfment in a fury of waters.

*Figure 11.* The final image of Hank Quinlan, "local police celebrity"—or..."God of the Smoking Mirror"?

relayed back from Jupiter by Voyager II of the diamond-studded moon, Callisto. This is in keeping with Welles' mystic practice: at key moments his image moves into the realm of surreality.

Abstractly viewed, this final image of Hank Quinlan, "local police celebrity," has the appearance of the three most vital facial orifices: the eyes and the mouth. And it is not impossible—indeed, it would require an act of willful avoidance of the obvious to deny it—to see in this figure's physiognomic correspondence a pre-Columbian skull mask in mosaic lignite and turquoise, with eye sockets of blackest obsidian, the Aztec supreme god, Tezcatlipoca, sky god of the four cardinal points, radiant Sun God of the South, and Black God of the North, god of the morning and evening stars. Tezcatlipoca—"God of the Smoking Mirror" wherein raged the war between night and day, god of mystic equipoise, the transcendent one, fusing the opposed forces of sky and earth, light and dark, time and space. (See Figure 11.)

*Touch of Evil* ends South of the Border—in the seedy little oil town of Los Robles—"the Oaks," sturdy, erect (though few have survived the incursion of Yanqui commerce).

We end with the death of an American cop, and his buddy. They broke the law—and must pay for their crime; this, the simplistic reading.

But there are levels on levels in *Touch*. It is a most remarkable film.

It is deep in a way only the greatest art is deep—in metaphysical reach.

For after this amazing final image of Hank-Tezcatlipoca, Tanya arrives, a late messenger (and it is not reading too much into this role which Dietrich claims is her favorite of all the roles she has played—and why should we doubt her word?) a late messenger from the gods. And her message, which an ancient Aztec shaman on the summit of the sacrificial pyramid might have uttered over his people's victim—an exemplary brave from an alien tribe whose heart was to be rent, in the fire of sacrifice to Tezcatlipoca, that the sun might be renewed— "He was some kind of man..."

But the human sacrifices in *Touch of Evil* bring no social renewal. The sun will not rise because of Hank's fall. Ours is not a great culture; materialism rules: oil rigs "pumping money," junk movies grinding out profits at the box office and on the tube.

And *Touch of Evil*, the masterwork of America's master filmmaker, world premiers on—a double bill, in Brooklyn yet.

There is no hope, no hope at all.

## Godard Moving
## in Crystal—"Weekend"

Irony lies in knowing ostensibly good fortune is less than that
and ill fortune is even worse than it seems. In brief, irony is
pessimistic in outlook.

It is the diametric opposite of sentimentality, which is based
on unfounded optimism.

Irony mocks conventional platitudes.

Ironic drama is against the American grain. The citizenry of
this land of opportunity don't cotton to naysayers. The American audience, the world audience, for that matter the mass
audience anywhere, likes to root for the hero, hiss the villain,
and smile at the happy ending.

So it is one will have to look hard and long to find an ironist,
much less a homegrown ironist, in American motion pictures.
In fact, one might make the drastic judgment that, aside from a
brief period at the end of that decade (the Sixties) in which the
American film audience came of age (before relapsing into the
sophomoric and soporific Seventies and the egregiously eczem-

atous Eighties), the American movie industry has been incapable of producing irony. One might even go so far as to claim that film did not achieve the plane of irony until the singular ironic note of Renoir in the Thirties found its resonant sounding board in the New Wave of the Sixties.

And, leading cinema into the ironic field, one filmmaker stands above the rest—Godard.

Indeed, the history of modern cinema might be encapsulated in a (perhaps groaning) play on Beckett: "Waiting for Godard."

It would not be too radical a dating system for modern cinema to adopt a Godardian calendar: B.G., G.(1959-68), and A.G.

Modern (read "ironic") cinema awaited a genius—Godard. The aesthetic and philosophic complexities of modern literature and thought found cinematic realization in his reflective and instinctual image structures: phenomenology and nihilism, quietism and brutalism, ontological presence and minimal absence, mannerism and primitivism, stringent structuralism and aleatory effects, solemn (and not so solemn) rites and deadpan pandemonium, classicism and Pop, reverent *hommage* and camp send-ups, conceptualism and Madison Avenue cliché, dogmatic dementia and metaphysical gnosis. You'll find it all there in the soft sculpture and earthwork museum without walls of the one, the only, Jean-Luc.

Quite simply, Godard is a miracle. Film in its largely tacky first century, did not earn his presence; it did not deserve his gifts. And now, looking back at his creative burst, 1959-68, one can only grieve that the world must turn, that times must change, and the excitement of the Sixties would, in the barrenness that has followed his absence in world cinema, seem, like the first decade of the 17th century for theater; or like the 1780's for Mozart, to be a height of cinematic energy that the medium shall never know again.

This isn't intended as a cultural history, but it does bear noting that the three ages of greatness in the arts coincided with times of radical change: the Jacobean rise of the wits, the final decay of the Bourbons and their elegance, and the advent of revolution against (as well as a hidden nostalgia for) bourgeois bad taste, narrow and mean, but also engagingly, campily, tacky. In laying out the three ages against which the new age reacted, side by side: the Elizabethan grandiosity, the Bourbon ultra-refinement, and the Eisenhower teduim (to say nothing of the tedious chaos of France in the fifties with its revolving-door chiefs of state), there is an all-too-evident drop in that definable something called style. It was the worst of times (or close to it), and it brought forth the best in Godard. He looked around him, between bouts at the cinematheque, at the maudlin mediocrity in its several guises and coolly averred:

> Film is life and a reflection on life: an adventure, with a philosophy of that life, say Husserl...
>
> (Godard in interview, with Michèle Manceaux, 1961)

Alluded to here, though the word may draw a blank with moviegoers, is the Marxian (Groucho) "magic word" that made Godard's screen light up, "phenomenology."

For an objective poetry of things, transformed by sheer joy in the filmic medium, is what makes Godard Godard; pure forms caught by the lens and timed on the movieola so as to catch the excitement (or delectable boredom) of "the moment."

All great directors are masters of form. What makes Godard phenomenal is his openness to the "adventure" of living (or living/dying), his reflective awareness that gives a charge of feeling to his forms. Images excite him, and the forms he finds are visually and aurally exciting.

This much said on Godard from a formal perspective, it has to be balanced by a recognition of his paradigmatic/metaphysical leanings.

*Figure 12.*

"Cover the flowers with flames," or
Godard Moving in Crystal

Gods moving in crystal...[1]
Ezra Pound

...artistic creation...[translates] the
mutable [into] crystalline form.[2]
Wilhelm Worringer

The geometric spirit distinguishes...the
subtle spirit of philosophy.[3]
Blaise Pascal

---

[1] Ezra Pound, Pisan Canto XCI (New York: New Directions, 1948).

[2] Wilhelm Worringer, *Abstraction and Empathy*, tr. Michael Bullock, (London: 1908; New York: International Universities Press, 1953), pp. 127, 134.

[3] Isabel F. Knight, *The Geometric Spirit* (New Haven: Yale University Press, 1968), p. 18.

*Figure 13.*

An innate schematism...[4]
...transforms force into structure.[5]
    Noam Chomsky, Gottfried Benn

Whole-natured creatures arise from the earth through
the separative action of fire.[6]
    Empedocles

    ...birds fly into the air because they are full
    of fire.[7]
        Aetius

---

[4] Ben Rothblatt, *Changing Perspectives on Man* (Chicago: University of
Chicago Press, 1968), p. 7.

[5] Gottfried Benn, "Nach dem Nihilismus," p. 21.

[6] Denis P. O'Brien, *Empedocles' Cosmic Cycle* (London: Cambridge University Press, 1969), p. 194.

[7] Ibid.

*Figure 14.*

We see by...the flash of our eyes mingling with
...the flash of the sun.[8]
  Plutarch

Gesture...rendering visible...the structural
rhythm.[9]
  James Joyce

  Do not be led away by the surface of things;
  in the depths everything becomes law.[10]
   Rainer Maria Rilke

---

 [8] Plutarch, "On the Cessation of Oracles," in *Selected Essays* tr. A.O. Prickard (Oxford: Clarendon Press, 1918). p. 167.

 [9] James Joyce, *Ulysses* (Paris: Shakespeare and Company, 1924), p. 425.

 [10] Rainer Maria Rilke, *Letters to a Young Poet,* tr., W.K.W. Maurer (London: Langley and Sons, 1943), p. 18.

*Figure 15.*

The world's moving power...cyclical movement...[11]
    Anaxagoras

The Beginning of Things...turning back on itself...[12]
    C. Kerenyi

            Nature geometrizeth.[13]
            Sir Thomas Browne

---

[11] Arnold Ehrhardt, *The Beginning* (New York: Barnes & Noble, 1968), p. 71.

[12] C. Kerenyi, *The Gods of the Greeks* (London: Thames & Hudson, 1951), p. 16.

[13] Sir Thomas Browne, "Garden of Cyrus."(1656)

*Figure 16.*

The major imperative of life is the articulation
of patterns.[14]
　　Radhakmal Mukerjee

...from the schema to the image.[15]
　　Henri Bergson

THE END OF CINEMA[16]
Jean-Luc Godard

Culture is a movement of the mind...from the void
toward forms, and from forms into the void...[17]
　　Antonin Artaud

---

[14] Radhakmal Mukerjee, *The Symbolic Life of Man* (Bombay: Hind
Kitabs, 1959), p. 32.

[15] Jean Paul Weber, *The Psychology of Art* (New York: Delacourt Press,
1969), p. 111.

[16] Jean-Luc Godard, *Weekend* (1968).

[17] Antonin Artaud, "Les Takahumaras," in Eric Sellin, *The Dramatic
Concepts of Antonin Artaud* (Chicago: University of Chicago Press, 1968),
pp. 202-04.

Movies, Godard has manifestly demonstrated, are much more than moving pictures. They are symbolic structures that move in the mind, and move the mind.

And what moved Godard?

Everything and anything, from the mundane to the (his word) "profound."

One of the qualities of Godard that annoys his detractors (and is vastly amusing to his followers) is his penchant for discovering "serious" (even "profound") value in the less than serious.

An instance, involving a red (lower case) shift (aesthetic, apolitical) is in the one feature he made on a big budget (for Carlo Ponti), *Contempt* (1963).

Predictably, in delivering the product, 110 pounds of feminine pulchritude, to his producer and the slavering world market, there is a scene (the opening one, to grab them early) with BB on a bed. Of it he has written:

> I used a red lighting, and then a blue lighting so that Bardot would become something else...more profound and more serious than simply Brigitte Bardot on a bed...
>
> (Godard, in interview with
> Yvonne Baby, 1963)

The "transfiguration" of BB may seem an extreme trope, yet the formal effect—and symbolic, as in the astrophysical shifts of celestial bodies—of the slow rhythmic pulse of color shifts over Bardot's epidermis to the throb of Mahlerish low strings fully justifies its extravagance.

Such intellectual-aesthetic reaching is a mark of Godard's work from its inception. *Breathless* (1959) is a dark rite beneath its gangster-genre surface. But in his works toward the culminating end of his creative flush (1967-68) the metaphysical reach became truly "profound." In *Two or Three Things I Know About Her* (1967), a glow of a cigarette over Gallimard *Idées'* book covers, suggests a supernova; a coffee cup, in extreme closeup, its sugar swirling and dissolving, becomes a galaxy lightyears away from the quotidian of its dramatic context, the Eliotesque ruminations (of Godard, whispered) adding verbal density to the cosmic moment:

> As I can neither free myself from the objectivity that is crushing me nor from the subjectivity which is driving me into exile...as it is impossible for me either to raise myself up to life or fall back into nothingness...I must...look around me attentively ...look at the world...

Awareness, a phenomenological key to presence, and to the Godardian *mise en scène*, going far beyond Husserl to Heidegger; most unusual, this: intellect as a key to a film director.

In *Weekend* there is another such metaphysical moment in the contemplation of a pebble. It is a still life, the frame fixing on the object. Yet the mind trained on the object is moving, across aeons, galaxies. The trajectory of his speculation on the pebble can only be inferred from its context: a meditation on the flames consuming "Emily Bronte"—"Cover the flowers with flames," and the closing image of the wife at the cannibal feast, gnawing on a bone that may well be the last mortal remains of her husband—"End of Cinema." It would seem that the pebble suggests dark thoughts of how far mankind has fallen from the unitary integrity of the pebble. Yet, beneath the earth upon which Godard stood, in his hymn to "Old Ocean" and the birth of life—and its dissolution in the fetal waters— there is, within a cave in Lascaux, in a deep cleft, an image inscribed upon the rock face of a fallen man. It is a stone that cannot be turned in the hand, immovable in its rigid stasis. Godard, in this most complex of his works (*Weekend*), would appear to deny such fixity of final stoppage. The process of regression in cannibal sacrifice here realizes the dream of another visionary, Antonin Artaud, and his theater of renewal.

Godard may invoke a Brechtian alienation-effect, inserting the title "End of Cinema" to terminate the drama. But it will not be stopped with a caption. To invoke the mythic dimension is to deny the surface appearance and to affirm the mystic dynamics of the psyche.

In this cannibal feast is the Bacchanalian echo of the revel rout. For *Weekend* is that rarest of ironic works, a seeming fall that is, in the deepest sense, a rise. *Weekend*, in this light, is a work of visionary cinema, going far beyond the spiritual inversions of Bresson; Godard's action involves an Artaudian metaphysical inversion, a transformational creation in annihilation.

"End of Cinema"? Or the beginning of the eternal journey of return?

The latter, I should propose; in the "End" man has not lost it all. Griffith (per C.B. DeMille) may have "photographed thought." Godard captures instinct, his arc of form fusing distant past and immediate present, Azilian lithic schema and Artaudian cinematic trope joining in an all-cancelling all-creating gesture.

"The End"? On the contrary, in Godard we have moving testimony "profound cinema" has just begun.

Yet no one picked up the traces when he let them fall. Godard has proven to be an impossible act to follow. As with Mozart, he had created classic forms of such contained intensity in a world that had little interest in fires on altars of the spirit and which, on his recession into a dry world of political dogma, continued on its mindless pursuit of topics and forms accessible to the mass "mind."

Less than two decades have passed since Godard was at his peak, yet looking back and considering his singular accomplishment, one has the feeling his oeuvre is an archeological dig, it seems so long ago.

No one in any art form has brought such freshness of vision

to his medium, and no one has been more alone—utterly alone. For though filmmakers in his wake (with the sole exception of Dušan Makavejev) have aped his techniques, none have grasped the inspired arc of his vision or the cold fire of his forms.

A conspectus of the energies driving this visionary reveals how much he gave his art in ten brief years.

## The Filmic Energy of Literature

Godard is literary.

He got into film by way of "reflection," writing criticism for the *Cahiers du Cinéma*. As he has said: "I consider myself an essayist, making films in the forms of essays." Thus he is aphoristic, much given to quotation from literature: the classics, pulps, fiction and non-fiction, poetry, essays, scientific studies; if it's in print, Godard might fit it in somehow, anyhow.

And he is anything but a snob in what he considers "literature" worthy of inclusion: comic strips and comic books are a major inspiration for his staging and dialogue, as well as his action ("Dick Tracy" in *Alphaville*, 1965). To Godard, the world is a "giant comic strip." Cardboard characters spout deep-think (and no-think) balloons of campy cliche. Also, advertising, magazine illustration, billboards, radio jingles, neon signs, signs of all kinds are cut into his action satirically, and, when words are partially masked, with intimations of the occult. Nor does he steer clear of the lowly pun. The play spirit is present, even in the most solemn context; in fact, the more solemn the context the more likely Godard will leaven the proceedings with something to jostle decorum.

## The Filmic Energy of Filmic Consciousness

Film-as-film; Godard reminds one frequently, and slyly, that "it's just a movie."

More than that, this filmic consciousness pervades his images and their structure, for Godard is well schooled in his art. Through long viewing at the Cinematheque he has a feeling for the masters and for the studio-director craftsmen. And, as well, he appreciates the differences in the feel of such technical matters as film stock, choosing to shoot *Band of Outsiders* (1964) on an Ilford still film stock so as to get the high contrast harshness suited to the barren wintry Paris environs of the film's setting; or cameras—favoring portable reflex jobs to make possible hand-held informality in the actional coverage.

## The Filmic Energy of Chance Action

Godardian film is aleatory, welcoming the accidental, chance event. Robin Wood has described *Weekend* aptly as "an accidental masterpiece." This quality arises as a result of Godard's famed looseness. He shoots quickly, depending often on serendipity to arrange things in some semblance of a coherent order, or perhaps not; no loss, order isn't everything.

Eccentric turns, these are to be expected in Godard. Quirks, foibles, bizarre behavioral tics, oddball shorting out of expected dramatic development, messages from out of left field (as well as Chairman Mao's Little Red Books—*La Chinoise*, 1967); in brief, chaos is come again in ways Othello might never understand, though Iago might, for they "do beguile...by seeming otherwise."

## The Filmic Energy of Fragmentation

Godard has observed: "The cinema is a world of fragments." And he has gone on to remark, "I like to shuffle the cards."

Famous for his "jump cuts" that leave out pieces of the action so it seemingly "jumps," such elision of the in-essential—or essential—imparts a staccato impetus to the frequently mad incongruities of sound and picture. Godard is a master of collage and frottage, pasting the detritus of everyday on his picture plane. Junk assemblages and cross-eyed compendia of the trivial and consequent; yet, amazingly it all hangs together. A cinematheque and bibliotheque with The Three Stooges as research consultants in Great Ideas—or Not-So-Great-Ideas, the random, shuffling of Mortimer Adler's and Harry Golden's notebooks interleafed with the wit and wisdom of W.C. and T.S.E.—to view Godard is to gain an education in the powers of association, and disassociation.

## The Filmic Energy of Continuum Action

At times, Godard will seemingly go out to lunch with the camera running. He'll pin nothing on the screen and hold on it till the viewer gets cross-eyed. He'll fix upon a *tableau vivant*, or a *tableau vacant,* so long it begins to stare back. Such extended takes can lend a remarkable scenic presence to the scene. Or it can be nothing short of boring. For, in Godard, boredom belongs. Droll inanity hath its charms (*Les Carabiniers*, 1963, starred two dunderheaded ninnies, based on Flaubert's *Bouvard et Pecuchet*, who disproved William Tecumseh Sherman's adage that "war is hell" and demonstrated that it can be just plain dumb).

## The Filmic Energy of Detachment

Godard's art is detached. He keeps a discreet, ironic distance, staying well clear of emotional involvement. He likes Mozart; no gummy Brahmsian strings underscoring the action for Jean-Luc, though, for his commercial international production starring Brigitte Bardot and Jack Palance, *Contempt*, he out-Steiner'd dear Max in overscoring in the strings the petty bickerings of his unhappy couple (Brigitte and Michel Piccoli). He prefers his poignance *tres sec*, as in Mozart's adagios: desolation with a lift.

## The Filmic Energy of Abstraction

To Godard, the world is a geometric figure, a kaleidoscope forming revelatory schemata. However banal, life is a pattern of vicious circles, straight lines to nowhere, eternal triangles or transient isomorphs, evanescent nexuses, blank walls, and meaningless vanishing points. In his "twenty-four-hour movie," a definition Godard has given for the way he views life, the animator could well be Saul Steinberg, for Godard's is a linear/alinear *camera stylo* calligraphy. Godard's schemata are self-destruct assemblages, protean jigsaws where every piece oddly fits or fits oddly.

Godard is a synoptic genius and contradiction in terms: an aphasic polymath who hears messages from galaxies not on any star chart. He is a poet, born out of his time, about three and a half centuries too late. For his is a metaphysical wit, "with a poet's eye, in a fine frenzy (or Fiat or Citroen or T-Bird) rolling, glancing from heaven to earth, from earth to heaven bodying forth the forms of things unknown..."

## The Filmic Energy of Openness

Godard is open to surprise; this the legacy of Renoir. He has followed the master's lead bid, and raised the ante. He opened up film through a Renoiresque loosening of the action both within the frame and between frames, and ventured further. He put into filmic action a principle alluded to previously, and it is a key one, uttered by that great Hollywood eminence C.B. DeMille. In extending the range of film from dramatic to thematic action, Godard realized what C.B. felt to be the key to the greatness of D.W. Griffith: "He photographed thought."

And therein lies the lesson in Godard: do not shoot action, nor reaction; be open to idea, or ideas.

The viewfinder frames life, fleeting images, still images, a blank screen, a black screen. Godard has said it: "Film is the only art that shows death at work."

"At work"—*energeia*: Godard.

*SCHEMA*

# Natural Philosophy and
# the Schema of Tragedy

Aristotle is the theorist of tragedy. He codified what had been created.

Anaximander is the inspirator of tragedy at Delphi's boundless center. He set forth the cosmic schema upon which classic tragedy is based.

Aristotle is tragedy's arbiter; Anaximander, its genius.

> Anaximander...was the first to depict
> ...Delphi...the navel of earth...at the
> center...[1]
> Charles S. Kahn

And, at the cosmic center of Delphi, Apollo thrice uttered

---

[1] Charles S. Kahn, *The Encyclopedia of Philosophy*, I (New York: Macmillan, 1967), p. 117.

the word. This we have from Aeschylus in *The Septem* (745-47).

Three is the number of fate, of the Fates who spin, measure, and cut the thread of life. And three is the basis for Anaximander's cosmic scheme: the depth of the earth three times its breadth, and the celestial bodies conforming to a triadic order—the fixed stars at a distance of nine times ($3^2$) the diameter of earth, the moon eighteen ($3^2$ x 2), and the sun twenty-seven times ($3^3$) the earth's diameter, or eighty-one ($3^4$) times its depth.

Three to the fourth power: the three dimensions of space, and the fourth of time—this is the schema of the Anaximandrian cosmos. Yet his inspired mind did not stop with the solar cosmos: he saw beyond—to "the Boundless."

Are we to believe that the center of his cosmos, Delphi, did not bear out his cosmic scheme? Archeologists have catalogued and plotted all the stones of the sacred center, but have divined no sacral order. To them it is a mere jumble. They have not discovered the secret order of its solar and astral orientation.

For Delphi is oriented toward the sun. It faces east in terms of a three-dimensional conceptualization of the seven-pointed star of light; and we recall that Apollo, its god, was "the Captain of Sevens."

The cosmic center at Delphi ordered space, and it ordered time, the calendar.

Originally the mantic seat at Delphi was held by Earth (Ge, Themis-Justice); then by Phoebe, the moon goddess, who ceded the seat to Apollo. Thus the moon is the central member of the Delphic succession, and "her" three phases the key to Delphi's mastery of time, of the calendar, for, as Theodore

Thass-Thienemann notes, "Moon derives from 'measurer,' "[2] as in the central member of the three Fates, Lachesis, the Measurer.

Here at the Anaximandrian center, the year was ordered into the three seasons, ushered in by the three Hours (Horae) borne by Delphi's first goddess, Themis, goddess of the hexagonally thrice-ploughed field.

And at the Anaximandrian center, in the temple of Apollo *and* Dionysus, the trieteric rite of the Bacchic Thiads was performed wherein the god of sacrifice was cut in three parts.

And at the Anaximandrian center of Delphi the second great Greek mind found order: Pythagoras spent one year at Delphi, at which time he "revolutionized the art of prophecy."[3] That Pythagoras was aware of Anaximander's cosmic scheme centered at the sacred seat of which he was an initiate we have from C.J. Vogel:

> The Pythagoreans put [number] over against Anaximander's [Boundless].... The combination of the two...the Pythagoreans called harmony.[4]

Here, at the Anaximandrian center of Delphi Pythagoras practiced his divine art of geometry, setting the center of the theater (Dionysus') at the precise distance and angle from the temple (Apollo's) center so an arc of 1/12th of the circle would precisely subtend the inner temple at the main entrance and the entrance to the inner sanctum. That Pythagoras was versed in astrological lore we have from Porphry: from Chaldaean seers

---

[2] Theodore Thass-Thienemann, *The Subconscious Language* (New York: Washington Square Press, 1967), p. 86.

[3] Spyros Meletzes and Helen Papadakis, *Delphi, Sanctuary and Museum* (Chicago: Argonaut, Inc., 1968), p. vii.

[4] C.J. Vogel, *Pythagoras and Early Pythagoreanism* (Assen: Van Gorcum, 1966), p. 242.

he gained insight into "the metaphysical principles of the cosmos."[5]

Here, within the templum, was observed the progression of the houses of the zodiac, a progress centered in the theater of Dionysus. That the great tragedians were aware of this cyclic drama centered in Delphi we might glean from a most curious cry from Cassandra (in Euripides' *The Trojan Women*, 328-29). Herein the mantic priestess "whirls," calling for Apollo to "lead the dance." And, in Sophocles' *Antigone* (1146), the Chorus sings of the fiery stars in its dance obeying the command of Dionysus. Apollo whirls, while Dionysus orders the stars in their circling course about the Delphic center.

Inscribed above the temple portal stood the mystic  $E$ , the fifth letter; in Pythagorean philosophy "five" symbolized marriage, as here at Delphi we have the "marriage" of Apollo and Dionysus. And within the temple stood the sacred tripod above the thrice-coiled serpent encompassing the navel stone of the cosmos; the tripod, three to the fourth power, a symbolic arrow penetrating time's mysteries. Here, within, was played out the prophetic drama in inspired hexameter, foretelling the course of man's destiny.

And, without, as though guiding the drama, the transit of the sun, lighting with its morning rays the Eastern pediment of Apollo and the nine Muses, of whom the ninth was Urania of Astronomy, lighting the tragic orchestra for the agon, and, as its rays faded on the Western pediment, Dionysus and the Thiades, passing into darkness.

And, in the darkness, above, the order of the night sky, of the stars.

And beyond the stars—the Anaximandrian Boundless.

This, the concept Anaximander conceived:

---

[5] Peter Gorman, *Pythagoras, a Life* (London: Routledge & Kegan Paul, 1979), p. 64.